JERUSALEM

I'd like to dedicate this book to my parents, Daphne and

the late Mervyn Millis, who taught me a love of books and

history, and to my wife, Rosanne, and sons Ben and Toby,

without whose patience, this would not have been possible.

THIS IS AN ANDRE DEUTSCH BOOK

This edition published in 2015 by Andre Deutsch
An imprint of the Carlton Publishing Group
20 Mortimer Street
London W1T 3JW

The content of this book was previously published in
Jerusalem: The Illustrated History of The Holy City

Text © Joseph Millis 2012
Design © Carlton Publishing Group 2012, 2015

A CIP catalogue record for this book
is available from the British Library.

ISBN 978 0 233 00461 7

Printed in China

10 9 8 7 6 5 4 3 2 1

JERUSALEM
THE STORY OF A GREAT CITY

JOSEPH MILLIS

ANDRE
DEUTSCH

CONTENTS

PREVIOUS PAGE A view of Jerusalem in the nineteenth century in a watercolour by Friedrich Perlberg.

OPPOSITE The shining city on the hill: a contemporary view of Jerusalem at sunset, through the eyes of the Israeli photographer Duby Tal, 2009.

INTRODUCTION

Jerusalem. **It is probably the most fought-over piece of real estate in the world.** Through its more than 3,000-year history, the city has been ruled by Canaanites, Jews, Assyrians (almost), Babylonians, Greeks, Romans, Muslim Arabs, Christian Crusaders (from modern France, Germany and other European countries), Byzantine Christians from today's Turkey, Muslim Turks, the British and then the Jews again. And still its status has yet to be finally determined.

During this long history, Jerusalem has been destroyed at least twice, besieged 23 times, attacked 52 times, and captured and recaptured 44 times. In his seminal book *Jerusalem: The Biography*, Simon Sebag Montefiore notes that for 1,000 years Jerusalem was solely Jewish, was Christian for around 400 years and then Islamic for 1,300 years and yet none of these faiths managed to gain control of Jerusalem without resorting to the use of weaponry. Few other cities have such a dark history of murder, rape, pillage and torture.

The oldest part of the city was settled in the fourth century BC, making Jerusalem one of the oldest continuously inhabited cities in the world. The old walled city is a UNESCO World Heritage Site.

Jerusalem is holy to the three Abrahamic monotheist religions Judaism, Christianity and Islam. It has an old, walled city divided into four quarters: Jewish, Christian, Muslim and Armenian. Yet outside the Old City walls, it is a bustling metropolis with a population of about 750,000 people, living in 652 square kilometres (252 square miles), making it the biggest city in Israel both in terms of the number of residents and its size. Jews make up about 65 per cent of the population; the remainder are Palestinian Arabs.

The city has top-class hotels, restaurants, shopping malls, orchestras, museums, basketball and football teams, a biblical zoo and a thriving cultural night life. It has recently introduced a light-railway system to help alleviate traffic problems – although, this being Jerusalem, there are political problems as the line goes through areas to the east and north of the city that the Palestinians want as part of their own capital.

For Jews, it is the holiest place on Earth, and devout followers of the faith pray three times a day in its direction. At Passover, the ceremonial meal or Seder is concluded with the cry "Next Year in Jerusalem". The Western Wall, last standing remnant of the Second Temple destroyed by the Romans in AD 70, is the holiest site in Judaism. There is, in Jewish lore, a temporal Jerusalem and a spiritual one, which hovers above the physical city.

The Talmud – the post-biblical rabbinic discussions on how to interpret the correct way to conduct Jewish law, ethics, philosophy, customs and history – teaches that: "Ten measures of beauty descended on the world – nine were taken by Jerusalem, one by the rest of the world. There is no beauty like the beauty of Jerusalem."

For Muslims, it is the faith's third most important place, after Mecca and Medina, because Muhammad travelled there on his night flight on his steed al-Buraq. The hoofprint of al-Buraq is supposedly seen in the rock in the gold-domed shrine known as the Dome of the Rock. Nearby, on what Jews call Temple Mount and Muslims term the Noble Sanctuary, is the silver-domed al-Aqsa Mosque, the third most important mosque for Sunni Muslims. Al-Aqsa means "the furthest", the site being the furthest place Muhammed reached as he spread Islam.

Jerusalem is the story of this region. Through stunning images and removable documents it brings alive this intriguing, beguiling, yet bloody and still fought-over city.

Joseph Millis

The Origins of Jerusalem

Jerusalem's origins lie in pre-biblical times, long pre-dating its settlement by the Hebrews, who rebuilt it and were to make it their capital and holy city. People had lived on the hills that would later make up Jerusalem from around 5000 BC – long before even the Bronze Age.

The first known mentions of the city were in around 2000 BC in the Middle Egyptian Execration Texts – in which the city was recorded as Rusalimum – and in the Amarna tablets, diplomatic correspondence from the reign of Akhenaten (c.1350 BC). S-L-M, the linguistic root of Rusalimum, is thought to refer to either "peace" (*salam* in modern Arabic, *shalom* in modern Hebrew) or Shalim, the deity whom the ancient Canaanites believed presided over the dusk.

The Amarna tablets are an archive of letters between the Egyptian pharaohs Amenophis III and his successor Akhenaten and other Near Eastern rulers. They were found in 1887 at Tell el-Amarna in Egypt (from which they take their name). The vast bulk of them were unearthed then, only 50 of the 382 numbered tablets coming to light subsequently.

The letters on the majority of the tablets date from the mid-fourteenth century BC. They cover correspondence with independent rulers of Babylonia, Assyria, Hatti and Mitanni, a variety of minor kings in the Near East, and vassal rulers of states in the area of modern Israel, Syria, Palestine and Lebanon.

This discovery and its rapid decipherment revolutionized scholars' understanding of the history and political development of the region. Those tablets representing letters from Canaanite rulers to Egyptian pharaohs were written in a mix of Canaanite and Akkadian, providing invaluable evidence of the dialects of Canaanite spoken around Jerusalem in pre-Israelite times.

BELOW Through the ages, water has always been a problem for the residents of Jerusalem. This sketch, from 1844, shows Jerusalemites drawing from the lower Pool of Gihon near the Old City walls.

J.W.WHIMPER

ABOVE A photograph, from around 1870, shows the tenth-century BC Jebusite fortress on Mount Zion inside which King David is said to be buried. Christians believe that the Last Supper may have taken place here.

Around this time, urban life in the area was flourishing. The city of Uruk in modern Iraq may have had a population as great as 40,000, while the walled town of Jericho, which had sprung up in an oasis north of the Dead Sea, was one of the main urban centres in the region. In the area of Jerusalem itself, settlements began to grow around burial areas in the surrounding hills, on the margins of the Judean Desert and in the vicinity of the spring of Gihon.

Evidence yielded by archaeological excavations indicates that monumental city walls – some eight metres (26 feet) high – were built by the Canaanites in the seventeenth century BC. Erected on the eastern side of the settlement, these protected the precious water channels that led from the springs of Gihon and Shiloach. The springs themselves were guarded by a huge, thick wall with stones weighing up to three tonnes.

During the period from 1550 to 1400 BC, Jerusalem fell under the hegemony of the early pharaohs of New Kingdom Egypt. Ahmose I (1570–46 BC) and Thutmose I (1525–12 BC), who had reunited Egypt, expanded its territory deep into the Levant (modern-day Israel, Lebanon, Palestine, Jordan and Syria), subordinating much of the area to their rule. Letters sent by Abdi-Heba, the headman of Urusalim (Jerusalem), to his Egyptian overlord Amenophis III (1417–1379 BC) and the picture we get is of a city which had grown sufficiently large and wealthy to support a significant skilled artisan class.

During the twelfth century BC, a series of attacks on the established power of the Late Bronze Age by groups known collectively as the "Sea Peoples" led to the eclipse of Egyptian power, which suffered a severe blow in 1178 BC at the Battle of Djahy (the Egyptian name for Canaan). Out of the ruins of central authority, a number of smaller independent kingdoms began to emerge in the region.

Jerusalem is first mentioned in the Bible in Genesis 14:18, when Abraham paid tithes – tax – to the King of Salem, Melchizedek. The name Jerusalem itself is not used, however, yet it seems likely to be the same place because Abraham was said to be in the area and the city's name Salem is part of its later name. According to one Jewish tradition reported by the *midrash* (the ancient Jewish homiletic method of biblical exegesis, which took a biblical event, law, tradition or personality and interpreted it beyond what is written in the actual text by using hints and nuances hidden in the text – the term also refers to the whole compilation of homiletic teachings on the Bible), Jerusalem was founded by Abraham's forefathers Shem and Eber.

Abraham went to Mount Moriah, just to the north of the Old City of Jerusalem, to offer Isaac as a sacrifice (Genesis 22:2). Later, Mount Moriah was incorporated into the city as Temple Mount and is where Solomon built his temple – the First Temple.

ABOVE Abraham is welcomed by Melchizedek to Salem, one of the
original names of Jerusalem according to this late-fifteenth-century
coloured woodcut by Michael Wolgemut from the *Nuremberg Chronicle*.

The name "Jerusalem" first appears in the Bible in the Book of Joshua (10:1), where the city's king Adonai-Tzedek fights against Joshua, but is defeated in the Valley of Ayalon. According to the biblical account, Jerusalem was conquered, sacked and abandoned to the Jebusites, who held it for 400 years until it was captured in 1003 BC by David, who annexed it and made it his capital (2 Samuel 5:6) of the United Kingdom of Israel.

One theory – probably the most likely – argues that the Israelites were outsiders who captured the area from the semi-Semite Jebusite tribe, which had lived there for generations. Another theory is that they arrived from Egypt after the exodus. However, since Canaan was part of the Egyptian empire of the time, it is likely that, as they could move about within its territory, at least some Israelites already lived in the area. Another theory has it that they were a sub-sect that developed in the Canaanite mountain-dwelling Jebusite tribe.

So how did the Hebrews alight upon the name Jerusalem – or Yerushalayim in their language? The reason may be simply that it could be easily transliterated into a form that had great significance in Hebrew. The final part seemed closely related to *shalom* ("peace"), a word whose root contains a sense of completeness or wholeness (also found in the names Solomon and Absalom). The first syllables of Jerusalem sound like the word *yara*, to throw, cast or shoot, a verb used for the loosing of arrows, hurling of stones and casting of lots.

It may be that the name Jerusalem was simply Hebraized, rather than changed, as it could mean "rain of peace" – another derivation of the word *yara* is *yoreh*, meaning first rain of winter. Jerusalem was to be the radiating heart of a world of completeness and wholeness, somewhat ironically for a city that has from time immemorial been caught up in almost constant conflict and strife.

OPPOSITE According to the Book of Genesis, Abraham offered up his son Isaac for sacrifice on Mount Moriah, which is just north of Temple Mount, before God ordered him to stop. Bible illustration painted by Philip de Bay, c.1860.

BELOW The prologue of the Hammurabi Code. The Babylonian code, from around 1770 BC, is the first known codification of laws pertaining to rights, duties and contracts.

THE HAMMURABI CODE

King Hammurabi was the sixth King of Babylon and ruled from 1792–50 BC. In around 1772 BC he compiled his legal code of Babylonian law – one of the world's first codifications of a legal system, and it probably predates biblical law. It was written on a large stone monument – also known as a stele – and placed in a public place so everyone could have access to it. It is currently in the Louvre, in Paris.

Like the Amarna tablets, the Hammurabi Code was written in Akkadian. It contains more than 280 laws written on 12 tablets and shows each offence and the punishment the offender had to pay for retribution. It is one of the first instances of *Lex Talonis* (an eye for an eye, a tooth for a tooth), but it is also clear on the use of evidence and the presumption of innocence.

King David and His City

Did King David, the monarch who unified the kingdom of Israel and centred it on Jerusalem, even exist? There were thought to be no contemporaneous accounts of his existence in Egyptian or Assyrian documents and many archaeological digs in Jerusalem – one of the most researched cities in the world – have failed even to find any mention of him.

However, in 1993, a team of Israeli archaeologists surveying the north of the country uncovered a triangular basalt rock inscribed in Aramaic from the ninth century BC. It refers to "The House of David" and this suggests that a king named David did indeed rule in the area and established a dynasty.

OPPOSITE David was a warrior king who expanded his empire from Jerusalem and the united Kingdoms of Judea and Israel, to an area covering most of the Levant and even Egypt. Here he is seen killing Philistines in the *Speculum Humanae Salvationis* or Mirror of Human Salvation, an illustrated book from the late Middle Ages on the subject of popular theology.

ABOVE A photograph taken around 1870 of the Jebusite Fortress and the surrounding buildings on Mount Zion. The buildings show how Jerusalem has been ruled by the three great Abrahamic religions, with a church and mosque as well as supposedly the tomb of King David, the Jews' warrior monarch.

Other digs have uncovered artefacts and inscriptions that suggest that Judea's population doubled in the eleventh and tenth centuries BC, and that its centre was Jerusalem. It is certainly not conclusive evidence for the existence of David, but it does suggest the establishment of a centralized state around Jerusalem at the time.

Nonetheless the balance of probabilities indicates that King David did exist and he made Jerusalem his capital some time in the tenth century BC. The American-born missionary and historian Edwin Thiele dates David's life to the mid-eleventh and tenth centuries BC, with his reign over a united Kingdom of Israel dated to 1003–970 BC.

The British officer Lieutenant (later General) Charles Warren of the Royal Engineers, was commissioned in 1867 by the Palestine Exploration Fund – which was set up to study the Levant and open Syria to Christianity – to conduct archaeological excavations around the Old City. Warren was a great friend of the Jews, and believed that they should re-establish their dominion over the land with the help and protection of the European powers.

As a result of to local opposition by Jews and Muslims, Warren was forced to hire plots of land near the Temple Mount where he sank 27 shafts and uncovered what were probably the first archaeological artefacts found in the city. One of the shafts, on Ophel Hill, he believed to be King David's conduit into the city.

According to the Jewish religion, David is a direct descendant of the Messiah, the anointed one. Jesus was born in Bethlehem – 10 kilometres (six miles) south of Jerusalem – the same city as David, and was said to have been from the same family. In Islamic tradition, Dawud – his name in Arabic – is a prophet and warrior king of his nation.

Israel's kings were chosen by the prophet, initially by Samuel. However, his first choice was Saul, a young warrior who was greatly troubled, in effect mentally unstable. Samuel looked elsewhere, and found David, one of the eight sons of Jesse of Bethlehem who was "ruddy and of beautiful countenance, and goodly to look to", according to the Book of Samuel.

Samuel brought David to Saul's court and the latter appointed him one of his top officers. David had another role; to play harp to Saul to calm him when the king was having one of his breakdowns.

When the Philistines were advancing on the kingdom, in the Valley of Elah, just south of Jerusalem, the Bible says that David, the young warrior, used his sling and hit the giant Goliath in the forehead, killing him. The Philistines took flight after that.

KING DAVID AND HIS CITY

Following this, Saul promoted David who became friendly with the king's son Jonathan and his daughter Michal. Saul allowed him to marry Michal, but tried to have his son-in-law killed twice out of jealousy.

David, having had enough of Saul's attempts to kill him, defected to the Philistines who gave him dominion over the town of Ziklag. The Philistines once again marched on Saul's army, defeating him at Gilboa in the north and killing Jonathan. Saul committed suicide.

The southern tribes of Judea anointed David king, while the northern tribes of Israel anointed Ishbosheth. A bitter war raged between the two kingdoms for seven years until Ishbosheth was murdered and the northern tribes made David their king, leading to a united kingdom.

Jerusalem was not David's first choice of capital – that honour went to Hebron, about 30 kilometres (19 miles) south of the Holy City. But as David was elected by both the northern and southern kingdoms, he needed a new capital that was central and fortified, very easy to defend and hard to conquer. Being sited on a hilltop, Jerusalem fitted the bill. And as David brought the spiritual symbol of the Ark of the Covenant to the city, Jerusalem gained significance as both a political and religious centre.

Jerusalem in David's day was minuscule. While Babylon at this time was about 2,500 acres, Jerusalem covered less than 20 acres. It had a population of about 1,200, with most of them living around David's citadel.

David was nothing if not a consummate strategist – and he was a very lucky leader, too. He was able to build an empire with Cretan, Philistine and Hittite mercenaries, stretching from today's Iraq in the north to Egypt (some say the length of the Nile) in the south. He took full advantage of geo-political shifts in the region that saw the decline of Egypt and Mesopotamia. All of this was in spite of Jerusalem being a very small city compared to other regional centres.

LEFT Most of what we know now about Jerusalem's ancient past comes from archaeological digs, like this one at the 3,000-year-old City of David excavation site in the mid-1980s.

ABOVE The City of David has mostly been uncovered, as this tenth-century-BC structure shows.

OPPOSITE A lot of the archaeological work in Jerusalem started in the mid-nineteenth century when Victorian explorers started to travel through Palestine. One such team was made up of (seated left to right): Lieutenant Charles Warren; Joseph Barclay, Third Anglican Bishop of Jerusalem; Corporal Henry Phillips. Reclining: Frederick W Eaton. Standing: Jerius, dragoman to the British Consulate.

David prepared the ground for the building of the First Temple, but was unable to do so, leaving the task to his son King Solomon. The Bible says (in 2 Samuel) that David was prevented from building the Temple because of his sins:

"When your days are done and you lie with your fathers, I will raise up your offspring after you... and I will establish his kingship. He shall build a house for My name, and I will establish his royal throne forever." (2 Samuel 7:12–13).

And:

"[The prophet] Gad came to David the same day and said to him, 'Go and set up an altar to the Lord on the threshing floor of Araunah the Jebusite... So David bought the threshing floor... And David built there an altar to the Lord and sacrificed burnt offerings and offerings of well-being."
(2 Samuel 24:18–25).

However, David purchased the land designated for the Temple and built an altar there to atone for his many sins, both of the flesh and of the mind.

According to Muslim tradition, David – who is one of Islam's prophets – bought the land on which the Dome of the Rock was built. This place, on Mount Moriah, is where Muhammad ascended to heaven during his night flight known as the *isra*.

CHARLES WARREN

As well as being an archaeologist and a soldier, General Sir Charles Warren, GCMG, KCB, FRS (1840–1927) also served as Commissioner of Police of the Metropolis from 1886–88. His biggest case during this period was undoubtedly that of Jack the Ripper. Warren received a great deal of criticism for his handling of the case and his ultimate failure to bring the killer to justice. He eventually resigned in November 1888 and returned to military service.

King Solomon's Temple

King David was unable to build the Temple in Jerusalem as he had desired. However, he laid the groundwork for his son Solomon to build what the Jews call the First Temple on Temple Mount (Mount Moriah or Zion or, according to Islam, The Noble Sanctuary).

According to the Bible, it stood from its construction in the tenth century BC to its destruction by Nebuchadnezzar II after the Siege of Jerusalem in 587–586 BC. In the sixth century AD, Gregory, Bishop of Tours, included the Temple on a list of seven wonders of the ancient word (the list also included the Pharos of Alexandria and Noah's Ark).

Previously, the Mount had been used before as a place of worship, possibly as a Jebusite sanctuary (belonging to the mountain-dwelling Canaanite tribe who occupied Jerusalem prior to its conquest by David). Before David united the northern and southern kingdoms in 1003 BC, the Temple Mount served the God of Israel and was where the Ark of the Covenant (the gold-plated box in which the tablets of the law brought down from Mount Sinai by Moses during the Exodus from Egypt were placed) was located.

Due to contemporary political and religious conflicts, there have been very few proper archaeological surveys of the Mount, and so there is no evidence that Solomon's Temple actually existed; the sole contemporaneous source for its existence is the Old Testament.

However, in 2007, the remains of artefacts were found dating from the eighth to sixth centuries BC, making them possibly the first physical evidence of human activity during the First Temple period. The findings included parts of jugs, bowls and other utensils, as well as animal bones.

In the Bible, in 1 Kings 6:1–38 and elsewhere, the construction and the dedication of the Temple is described in great detail. King Solomon asked his northern neighbour King Hiram of Tyre to supply the materials, such as fine cedar wood, and to find skilled craftsmen to build this magnificent building.

Solomon expanded his empire through trade with Egypt and Cilicia – today's southern Turkey – from whom he got spices, chariots, gold and horses. He sent out trading expeditions to Sudan and Somalia with King Hiram of Tyre, his great ally to the north. He also hosted the Queen of Sheba, from the southern tip of the Arabian peninsular, who brought to Jerusalem camels laden with spices, gold and precious stones.

ABOVE King David was not able to build the Temple, but he brought the Ark of the Covenant to the city of Jerusalem when he made it his capital, as depicted in this work by William Brassey Hole, c.1925.

His House of God benefited greatly from these beautiful gifts and bounty. It stood next to his palace. Its building, not just a shrine but a home for God, served as a testimony to the co-operation between the peoples of the area. It took a total of seven years to complete and when it was finished, all the residents of Jerusalem gathered to watch the priests carry the acacia wooden chest of the Ark of the Covenant from its tent in the citadel to the Temple and into the Holy of Holies (called the Kodesh Hakodashim in Hebrew), the inner sanctum, that had been built during the construction to house the Ark of the Covenant. It stood here alone, save for two cherubim.

Although it is generally accepted that the Temple was on Mount Moriah, the exact position of the Holy of Holies is disputed (and that is one of the main reasons that to this day, ultra-Orthodox Jews are not allowed to go up on the Mount for fear of desecrating the place where the Ark was located). According to one account, the stone altar that stood at the centre of the Holy of Holies is where the Dome of the Rock is, with the rest of the temple to the west. Another theory puts it between the Dome of the Rock and the al-Aqsa Mosque. This is based on the position of drainage channels, orientation of the platform stones and the location of a possible pillar base.

ABOVE The Temple was built by David's son Solomon and this nineteenth-century wood engraving shows the king overseeing the construction.

ABOVE Under Solomon, Jerusalem became a centre for royal visits. Among those who travelled to the city was the Queen of Sheba. This bronze panel depicting Solomon greeting the queen, completed in 1452 by Lorenzo Ghiberti, is located on the doors of the Florence Baptistry in Italy.

In the end, wise King Solomon became a tyrant who imposed huge taxes to fund more and more outlandish schemes which reduced his credibility. As his popularity waned, he faced rebellions from the far flung corners of his kingdom and his local religious leaders castigated and criticized him for indulging in idolatry and adultery. He died, in 930 BC, after 40 years on the throne, and was succeeded by his son Rehoboam.

The Temple's construction – or perhaps the myths about its construction – have inspired many latter-day scientists, among them Sir Isaac Newton, who would write extensively on the subject. An entire chapter of his book *The Chronology of Ancient Kingdoms* is dedicated to the Temple, for example. The Freemasons base their membership on a fraternity of those who know the secret of the construction of King Solomon's Temple.

Since the people who wrote the Bible were neither architects nor engineers, the Old Testament lacks technical details. However, according to Talmudic sources, the three-storey-high Temple was 30 metres (100 feet) long, 10 metres (33 feet) wide and 15 metres (50 feet) high. It had a cedar roof, overlaid with pure gold. It was east-facing and had a porch at least 10 metres (33 feet) long, although some estimates put the latter longer and higher.

The stone for the building was prepared off-site so as not to desecrate the surroundings. Inside, the perfectly cuboid Holy of Holies, which was separated from the rest of the Temple by a silk veil, had olive-wood cherubim about 15 metres (50 feet) high. The main part of the Temple, lined with cedar, had carvings of cherubim, palm trees and flowers, all of which were overlaid with gold. There were also two bronze pillars, named Jachin and Boaz.

The Temple underwent several changes, especially after the seventh-century-BC King Menasseh (687–643 BC) introduced idols to the building. His grandson King Josiah removed the idols and destroyed the priesthood that had grown around this form of worship.

Babylonian King Nebuchadnezzer II ransacked the building in around 598 BC when Joachim was on the throne. He then destroyed it totally in 586 BC, on the inauspicious Jewish date of the 9th of Av. This date is notorious in Jewish history, as it is when the Second Temple was also destroyed, this time by the Romans, more than 650 years later. Several other calamities have befallen the Jewish people on that date, including the expulsion of Spain's Jews in 1492 and a terror attack on a Jewish community building in Buenos Aires, Argentina, in July 1994 (an atrocity which killed 86 and wounded 300 others).

ABOVE The Madaba Mosaic Map, found on the floor of St George's Church in the town of the same name in Jordan, places Jerusalem at the centre of the world. It dates from around the sixth century CE.

The Assyrians and the Babylonians

Under the ruthless leadership of Sennacherib (705–681 BC), the Assyrians expanded their territory dramatically in the Near East, driving out the Greeks who were in the process of establishing a foothold in Cilicia (a region which extends inland from the south-eastern coast of modern Turkey, where it meets today's Syria) and in the north-eastern part of Cyprus. As part of his creation of an Assyrian empire, Sennacherib also swept through Israel and Phoenicia, where the Egyptians had tried, unsuccessfully, to entice the inhabitants into an anti-Assyrian revolt.

In the process, Sennacherib ravaged the Assyrian province that had formerly made up the northern kingdom of Israel and established a stranglehold over the southern kingdom of Judah, dominating much of the Levant, including Phoenicia and Aram (Damascus).

At the time of the fall of the northern kingdom, in around 720 BC, Judea was ruled by joint kings Ahaz and his son Hezekiah. In order to re=tain some independence and to stave off an Assyrian onslaught, Judah paid an annual tax to Sennacherib.

After the death of Ahaz in 715 BC, Hezekiah became King of Judea and reformed religious practices – especially removing the idols that Ahaz had introduced, reinstalling the monotheist belief the Jews had previously held. A warrior king, Hezekiah recaptured the Philistine-held lands in what is now Israel's Negev desert and southern coastal plain. He also formed an alliance with Egypt.

Yet Ahaz made a fatal error in refusing to pay the annual tax to the Assyrian Empire. Furious, Sennacherib attacked Judah and laid siege to Jerusalem in 701 BC.

However, despite his armies' numerical strength and the weakness of the city's defenders, Jerusalem did not fall to Sennacherib. No one knows quite why, but a number of conflicting accounts explain how this happened.

The siege is recalled in the Books of Isaiah, Chronicles and the Second Book of Kings. Hezekiah made careful preparations to defend Jerusalem, blocking the few springs outside the city to deny the Assyrian armies access to fresh water – absolutely vital in desert warfare. A tunnel more than 500 metres (1,650 feet) long was excavated by hand through solid rock to the Gihon Spring, to ensure the city's fresh water supply was maintained. The winding tunnel was rediscovered only in the nineteenth century, when two Arab schoolboys entered and followed it to its exit in the Old City.

The city's existing walls were fortified, towers were constructed and a new wall built behind the old one. Hezekiah gave a rousing speech to his people telling them the Assyrians possessed only an "arm of flesh" while they had divine protection.

Hezekiah dammed a valley to the north of the Temple Mount, creating the Bethesda Pools. This allowed the city to accumulate enough water to withstand a long siege. He also prepared the population and his troops for the coming onslaught by distributing oil, food and wine and poisoned wells outside Jerusalem in a further bid to deprive any advancing enemy of the vital resource of water.

There then began a bout of what today we would call psychological warfare. The field commander of the forces besieging Jerusalem conveyed a message to Hezekiah from Sennacherib, which was read out to the people guarding the city walls. Hezekiah's soldiers were told that their king could do nothing and that the God of Israel could not save them or Jerusalem from the wrath of Assyria.

Despite Hezekiah's anguish, the story is that the Prophet Isaiah assured the Judean king that the city would be saved and Sennacherib killed. The Old Testament relates that at some point, 185,000 Assyrians troops died in one night – the Bible saying that this was the work of the Angel of Death sent by God. Sennacherib retreated and Jerusalem was saved.

Hezekiah died soon after the siege was over and was succeeded by his son Menasseh. He was a brutal king and crushed any opposition to his rule. He brought idolatry to the Temple, introducing Baal and Asherah. Menasseh encouraged the sacrifice of children – by burning them alive – in the

Valley of Hinnom, just outside the city's walls. Hinnom inspired the vision of hell and in Hebrew and Arabic, the words for Hades are respectively Gehenom and Gehenna, a bastardization of Valley of Hinnom.

Unsurprisingly, the Assyrian account of the events is rather different. The Taylor Prism and the Sennacherib Prism, clay prisms which date from about 690 BC, are engraved with the annals of Sennacherib. They were discoverd in 1830 in Ninevah's ruins and boast how Hezekiah was trapped in Jerusalem "like a caged bird". The hasty withdrawal, however, is described as a glorious and victorious return to Nineveh after Sennacherib had been given a large sum of money from the Judeans. There is, of course, no mention of the death of 185,000 soldiers.

While there is no archaeological confirmation of either account, the Biblical story is partly corroborated by the Greek historian Herodotus and Jewish-turned-Roman historian Josephus Flavius. According to Herodotus in his *Histories*: "There swarmed by night upon their enemies mice of the fields, and ate up their quivers and their bows, and moreover the handles of their shields, so that on the next day they fled, and being without defence of arms great numbers fell."

Sennacherib's military adventures were expensive and they sapped Assyria's strength, allowing a rival force to arise in the east, a newly resurgent Babylon under Nebuchadnezzar II (604–562 BC). The Babylonian ruler tried to impose his rule over the region through a series of invasions, some more successful than others. His aggressive tactics led to numerous rebellions in the Levant including in Judah.

Nebuchadnezzar was ruthless in his pursuit of empire and captured Jerusalem in around 597 BC, after which he deposed King Jehoiachin. Ten years later, with the rebellion still bubbling under, he destroyed Jerusalem and laid waste to the Temple, expelling most of the Jewish population – especially the rich and talented – to Babylon.

According to the *Babylonian Chronicles*, contemporaneous texts that are now in the British Museum, "[I]n the seventh year [of Nebuchadnezzar, 599 BC] in the month Chislev [November/December] the king of Babylon assembled his army, and after he had invaded the land of Hatti [Syria/Palestine] he laid siege to the city of Judah. On the second day of the month of Adar [16 March] he conquered the city and took the king [Jeconiah] prisoner. He installed in his place a king [Zedekiah] of his own choice, and after he had received rich tribute, he sent forth to Babylon."

Babylon's great regional rival Egypt courted Zedekiah. The prospect of Zedekiah's defection worried

OVERLEAF The Babylonian ruler Nebuchadnezzar II was a ruthless leader who sacked Jerusalem and exiled the Jews. This iconic painting of him was produced by William Blake, circa 1795.

Nebuchadnezzar, who summoned him to Babylon to secure an assurance of his loyalty to him. But by the ninth year of his reign, Zedekiah had aligned himself with the Egyptians and rebelled against Babylon. Nebuchadnezzar did not take kindly to this and dispatched his army to stop the rebellion.

After the Egyptians intervened on behalf of their smaller ally, the Babylonians raised the siege long enough to repulse the Egyptians. Having seen off the Egyptians, the Babylonians returned to Jerusalem and within 18 months, its wall fell and Zedekiah and his sons fled towards the east, but were captured. Nebuchadnezzar showed no mercy – the sons were slain and Zedekiah was taken in chains to Babylon after the soldiers gouged out his eyes.

Whatever was left standing of Jerusalem was razed to the ground and the sacred vessels of the Temple were taken to Babylon. The city remained desolate and the Jews were not to return to Jerusalem for 50 years, in 538/7 BC after the fall of Babylon to the Persian king Cyrus the Great, who allowed the Jews to return to Jerusalem and rebuild their Temple.

BELOW Much of what we know about Nebuchadnezzar's destruction of Jerusalem is from the writings of Flavius Josephus. This image entitled "The Siege of Jerusalem by Nebuchadnezzar", is an illustration from the c.1470–76 French translation of Flavius Josephus's original manuscript.

OPPOSITE By the Rivers of Babylon: after Nebuchadnezzar destroyed the Temple, he exiled the Jews to Babylon. This nineteenth-century engraving by Gustave Doré shows the people of Jerusalem mourning over their conquered city, taken by the Babylonians in 586 BC after a 16-month siege.

BELOW Sennacherib, King of Assyria, who succeeded his father Salmanaser in 712 BC. In his time, Assyria was the greatest empire in the east, with Nineveh as its capital city. Sennacherib took several fortresses and laid siege to Jerusalem, but his army was slain in the night and he was forced to return to Nineveh. There he was murdered by his two sons as he was worshipping in the temple of the god Nisroch.

KING SENNACHERIB

Sennacherib (?–681 BC) dubbed himself "King of the World, King of Assyria" and he saw conquest as almost a religious duty, his position not only being military commander but high priest too. His empire stretched from the Persian or Arabian Gulf to Cyprus. When he recaptured Babylon, he destroyed it, razing it to the ground in order to build it anew. Archaeologists have found records of Sennacherib's achievements and the expansion of his empire through conquest and agriculture. In the royal archives are records of decisions taken and the religious help needed to take those decisions. There are even records of medicine prescribed for various ailments.

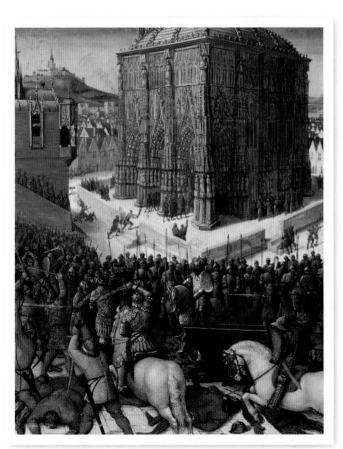

From Cyrus to Alexander

The Persian king Cyrus the Great (576–530 BC) is revered by the Jews because his conquest of Babylon ended their 50-year exile in that city and allowed them to return to Jerusalem in 539 BC. Some saw him as a messiah sent by God. The Old Testament mentions him by name no fewer than 23 times and he is alluded to several times more. In 530 he lead about 43,000 exiles back to the city.

The Cyrus Cylinder, a clay cylinder inscribed in Babylonian cuneiform with an account by the King of Persia of his conquest of Babylon in 539 BC and the capture of Nabonidus, its last king – now in the British Museum – refers to the return to their homelands of several displaced cultural groups, one

of which could have been the Jews, while Isaiah 41:2–4 also has an account of the Jewish return from exile. The Hebrew prophet, in chapter 45 (verses 1–3), also expresses the belief that Cyrus is doing the work of God, thus making him a messiah of sorts.

Cyrus's view of empire was in stark contrast to the Babylonians'. Where the latter expanded their empire through slaughter and deportation of indigenous populations, Cyrus offered religious tolerance in an attempt to acquire friends and influence people.

Cyrus appointed Sheshbazzar, the son of the last king, as governor of Jerusalem and returned the Temple's vessels

OPPOSITE This illustration from the fourteenth-century *Bible Historiale* shows King Darius being reminded of his promise to rebuild Jerusalem and return the Jews from their Babylonian exile.

LEFT In this illumiated manuscript from a sixteenth-century French Bible, King Cyrus is shown granting permission to a group of exiles to rebuild the Temple.

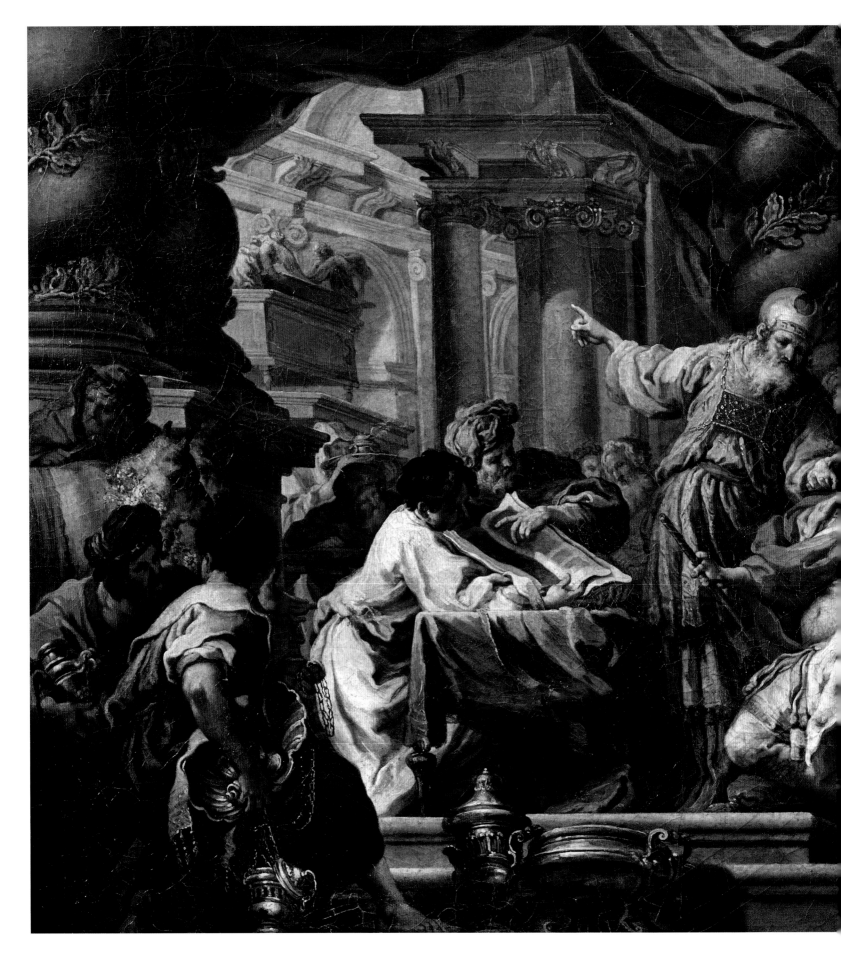

to him. For the dedication of the Temple, another Jewish prince, Zerubbabel, hired artesans and bought cedar wood from Phoenicia. For some Jews this was a sign of the advent of a messianic era, and Jews arrived from all over the empire bringing gold and silver in anticipation of the event.

Cyrus's decision to allow the rebuilding of the Temple in Jerusalem angered some of the non-Jews who lived in and around the city, and also those Jews who had not been exiled to Babylon and who did not recognize the Judaism of those who were returning. Some, to the north of the city, hired advisers who exhorted Cyrus and his successors Darius I (522–486 BC) and Artaxerxes II (465–424 BC) to delay the rebuilding. But, under Darius, the work recommenced because when the authorities asked the Jews what right they had to build a temple, they referred to the decree of Cyrus, which had to be found in the archives at Ahmetha in today's western Iran.

In 515 BC, the Second Temple was dedicated by the priests, led by Zerubbabel, who sacrificed 100 bullocks, 200 rams, 400 lambs and 12 goats – to signify the 12 Tribes and their sins. According to contemporaneous writing, despite the opulence and beauty of the Second Temple, it was a pale imitation of Solomon's and those who knew both buildings shed tears at the dedication.

Questions have been raised as to why Cyrus allowed the Jews back and permitted them to rebuild the Temple. The most prominent answer is probably that Cyrus was an adherent of Zoroastrianism, the Persian-based monotheistic faith that followed the teachings of Zoroaster. As the Jews also believed in a single god, Cyrus might be expected to have felt an affinity to them. He was also known to be open-minded towards, and tolerant of, other people's customs and beliefs. Even when he vanquished Babylon, he paid homage at the temple of the Babylonian god Marduk, thus gaining the support of the Babylonians and minimizing further bloodshed.

In 444 BC, during the decline of the Persian Empire, King Artaxerxes named his cup-bearer Nehemiah as governor of Judea, granting him funds and soldiers. Because of the decayed state of the city's walls, he demanded that each landowner and priest was given responsibility of a certain section of the wall to rebuild. Woe betide anyone who failed to fulfil his work and the reconstruction was completed in 52 days.

LEFT After the Babylonian and Persian conquests, a new power rose in the Near East, Alexander the Great. This eighteenth-century painting by Italian artist Sebastiano Conca shows the Macedonian ruler at the Temple in Jerusalem.

Nehemiah also ensured that Jerusalem's population would grow by holding lots for Jews outside the city. One in every 10 of those who drew the lots settled in the city.

When he travelled to Persia to report his progress in strengthening Jerusalem, the Samarians from the north started running affairs in the Temple while the local Jews started marrying non-Jewish tribesmen and women. Nehemiah, on his return, stamped down on this, expelled the Samarians and forbade intermarriage. He also introduced a stricter, purer Judaism.

The Achaemenid Persian empire eventually overstretched itself, and was conquered by the Macedonian Greek Alexander the Great in 335–330 BC. Alexander the Great's visit to Jerusalem is recorded by the Jewish-Roman historian Josephus Flavius in his *Antiquities*. He writes that Alexander visited the city after conquering Gaza and that Jaddua, the high priest, had envisaged that Alexander would adore the God of Israel.

Alexander then gave the high priest his right hand, and went into the Temple and "offered sacrifice to God according

LEFT A fifteenth-century illustration of Alexander the Great visiting Darius, King of Persia, in the fourth century BC.

THE DEATH OF CYRUS THE GREAT

According to Histories by Herodotus, Cyrus died in battle. Cyrus wanted to expand his territory and approached Tomyris, the ruler of the Massagetae tribe, with an offer of marriage, which she rejected. Cyrus then forcibly took the territory. Tomyris promised to avenge the Massagetae and led her troops into battle, this time killing Cyrus in 530 BC. Herodotus believed this was the bloodiest battle Cyrus had experienced. As an act of revenge, Tomyris had Cyrus decapitated and dipped his head in blood.

BELOW The death of Cyrus II, King of Persia, in 529 BC. In his nineteenth-century German steel engraving Queen Tomyris dips the head of Cyrus in a bowl of blood.

to the high priest's direction", treating the whole occasion with huge honour.

For the most part, life changed little for the people of Jerusalem under the Greeks – except in one crucial way. The rise of Alexander led to the Hellenization of the region and Greek culture became as pervasive then as American ways are now. Greek culture was king, and Jews and non-Jews alike in Jerusalem tried to emulate its poetry, language, religion and sport. Later this was to cause a Jewish civil war in Judea, of a sort that has not been seen before or since.

The Western Wall

When the Romans destroyed the Second Temple during the Jewish Revolt in AD 70, only one outer wall remained standing. However, because they considered it insignificant – it was not part of the Temple, it was just a surrounding wall – they left what was to become the Western (or Wailing) Wall standing. But for Jews, whether they are ultra-Orthodox or ultra-secular, the 488-metre (1600-feet) long, 56-metre (184-feet) high wall is the holiest spot on earth, to which they pray three times a day.

Just over half the wall, including a series of tunnels and pathways that are located below street level, date from the end of the Second Temple period, commonly believed to have been constructed around 19 BC by Herod the Great. However, recently it emerged that the works were not finished during Herod's lifetime. In 2011, archaeological excavations uncovered an ancient ritual bath near the Old City's drainage system. This ancient bath – or Mikve, in Hebrew – was built after the Herodian era, challenging the conventional wisdom that the Wall was built entirely during the king's rule.

BELOW The most sacred site in the world for Jews is the Western Wall, the last remnant of the Second Temple. This 1929 photograph shows Jews praying at the Wall.

The growing importance of Jerusalem – and especially of the Temple Mount – as a place of pilgrimage is demonstrated by the amount of reinforcement and maintenance work that were done on roads around the holy sites approximately 2,000 years ago. The archaeological excavations have found that the course of the drainage system, fully underground, stretched all the way from the Siloam Pool in the City of David to what is now an archaeological garden near the Western Wall itself.

According to the Israel Antiquities' Authority's archaeologists who conducted the dig, the remains discovered were from different periods. Some belonged to people who lived in the area before Herod decided to expand the Temple, which the contemporaneous historian Flavius Josephus described it as the biggest building project in the world at the time. During the excavations, the archaeologists found that the ritual bath, discovered in line with the Western Wall, contained coins and oil lamps that were used after the Herodian era and which come from the era of Valerius Gaius, who was procurator of Judea in the years AD 17–18. This led them to conclude that at least part of the Temple expansion was concluded in AD 17 or AD 18, at least 20 years after Herod met his very painful and gory death (thought to be around 4 BC).

This also means that Robinson's Arch (part of a stairway up to the Second Temple from the south-western corner of Temple Mount) – and the part of the Western Wall nearby – were built later than Herod. Josephus also noted that after the project was completed, the ranks of Jerusalem's unemployed swelled to more than 8,000 people.

Nowadays, the area around Robinson's Arch is used by those groups in Judaism called Progressive – Reform and Conservative Jewry – who do not accept the teachings of the Orthodox. They run the services at the Wall itself. In non-Orthodox Judaism, it is common to see men and women praying together and even women rabbis leading prayers. In Orthodoxy, on the other hand, there is strict gender separation and services can be led only by a male rabbi.

Today, the Western Wall attracts thousands of visitors a day. Some go to pray, or to take part in family celebrations, while others just stand there, marvelling at the Wall's construction and history.

Anyone going close to the Wall will see little white pieces of paper stuck between its cracks. The pieces of paper have prayers written on them by visitors who believe that they will go straight to the Almighty. These are prayers for the health of loved ones, for fortune and for peace. The practice is so popular that twice a year – before Passover and Jewish New Year – the authorities remove the little pieces of paper and store them nearby.

The Israeli postal authorities have also set up a post box for people to send prayers to, and there is even a fax and an email address. Some Orthodox Jewish groups have set up webcams on the Wall so their supporters can see what is going on there 24 hours a day.

Unfortunately, the Wall has been the scene of violence too – during riots, Muslim worshippers up on the Temple Mount have thrown stones on the Jews below.

And there is a rickety bridge between the Western Wall Plaza and the Temple Mount, the Mughrabi Bridge which no one dares fix despite fears of imminent collapse. To do so would be to spark a religious war.

RIGHT The Western Wall as it is now, with a plaza to accommodate the thousands of worshippers and visitors who arrive everyday. To make way for the plaza, Israel took down the Mughrabi Quarter, displacing 100 Arab families.

Egyptian-Greek and Roman Rule

When Alexander the Great died in 323 BC, his empire suffered a vicious civil war that resulted in the emergence of two main warring factions – the Seleucids in the North and the Ptolemies in the South. Caught in the middle was Palestine – and at its centre, Jerusalem – and it became the source and site of constant conflict. For around the first 100 years after Alexander's death, the Ptolemies were in control of Palestine. The first ruler was called Ptolemy Soter, who adopted a policy of transporting Jews from Palestine to Egypt, where they soon adopted Greek as their native language – an issue which, in the future, would become a source of internal Jewish conflict in Palestine.

The second Ptolemaic ruler Ptolemy II Philadelphus (285–246 BC) allowed the high priest, a council of priests and elders a degree of self-rule in Palestine, and as long as they paid an annual tax – or tribute – of 20 talents, they were more or less alone. Under Ptolemy II, the Bible was translated into Greek, a translation known as the Septuagint or LXX that would become the most popular version of the Old Testament among diaspora Jews.

These developments took place against a backdrop of continuing conflict between the Ptolemies and Seleucids. A temporary truce arose out of the marriage in 252 BC between Ptolemy II's daughter, Berenice, and the Seleucid ruler Antiochus II, but it was of brief duration and conflict between the two dynasties continued to simmer sometimes descending into outright war.

In 221 BC, Ptolemy III died and was succeeded by Ptolemy IV Philopater, who was without a doubt the most cruel and vicious of the Ptolemaic rulers. He hated the Jews and persecuted them without mercy. He even attempted to force his way into the Holy of Holies in the Jewish Temple and thus defile it. When he died, in 203 BC, Jerusalem's Jews celebrated.

The last Ptolemy to rule Palestine and Jerusalem was Ptolemy V Epiphanes (the "Illustrious") – although the dynasty did not end until 30 BC when Cleopatra died. In 200 BC, the Seleucids, under Antiochus III, took control of Palestine at the Battle of Panion in the Jordan Valley. They held the region until the Romans invaded in 63 BC.

The first time the Jews of Jerusalem felt the harsh hand of Seleucid rule – which they initially welcomed since it brought

ABOVE Soter Ptolemy I (367–283 BC). He was one of Alexander the Great's greatest generals and was King of Egypt from 323 BC.

to an end the constant warring with the Ptolemies – was when Antiochus III ("the Great") died in 187 BC and was succeeded by Seleucus IV. Antiochus had suffered defeats at the hands of the Romans and his successor was forced to pay fantastic amounts of tribute to Rome. To raise this money, Jerusalem's Jews were taxed heavily.

Some felt it was morally correct to give money to the pagan government of Rome, whereas others felt that to do so would be sinful, and two opposing factions formed among the Jews over the issue. The anti-Seleucid group formed around the high priest Onias, and became known as the Oniads. Opposing them was a group led by Onias's own brother, Jason, who sought to undermine Onias's position by making a series of false reports to Seleucus IV, hoping in this way that he would secure the position of high priest for himself.

But in 175 BC, Antiochus IV, also known as Epiphanes, murdered Seleucus IV and took the throne. He immediately took advantage of Jason's offer, and removed Onias, installing the brother in his place. Three years later, Jason's henchman Menelaus betrayed Jason by offering him even more money, and so secured his master's deposition and his own installation as high priest.

At the time there were Jews in Jerusalem who felt this corruption and bribery was a betrayal of their religion and faith in one God. They were called the Chasidim ("the pious"), and they renamed Antiochus "Epimanes" ("the madman").

When Antiochus invaded Egypt, in 169 BC, the Jews of Jerusalem were told he had been killed in battle. Upon hearing the news, the deposed high priest Jason, returned from exile and threw Menelaus out of the Temple and resumed his former lofty position. But Antiochus had not been killed and when he returned to Jerusalem, defeated but very much alive, Jason was thrown out of the city and Menelaus was reinstalled. To compound the insult, Antiochus raided the Temple and stole a great deal of valuable treasure.

In 168 BC, Antiochus went to Egypt again, but this time the Romans intervened on the side of the Egyptians, halting his invasion, and his life was spared only after he promised never to try and invade again. Antiochus was so angered by this setback, that, upon his return to Jerusalem, he tore down the city walls, put a great number of the inhabitants to the sword, ordered the destruction of Jewish scriptures, and defiled the Temple by allowing his soldiers to bring prostitutes into it. He ordered everyone to worship the Greek gods, and he established the death penalty for anyone who practised circumcision, or who observed the Sabbath, or any of the Jewish religious feasts and sacrifices.

The cruelty of Antiochus in enforcing these new laws against the Jews became legendary. An aged scribe by the name of Eleazar was flogged to death because he refused to eat pork. In another incident, a mother and her seven young children were butchered in the presence of the governor for refusing to worship an idol. In yet another incident, two mothers, who had circumcised their newborn sons, were driven through the city and then thrown to their deaths from the top of the city's wall.

The final outrage for the Chasidim came when Antiochus sacked the Temple and erected an altar there to Zeus, offering a pig as sacrifice. This sparked a large-scale rebellion of the Jews against the Seleucids, the Maccabean Revolt.

The leader of the revolt, Mattathias the Hasmonean, killed a Jew who had been supportive of the Seleucids. When Antiochus's forces came after him, he and his five sons fled to the Judean Desert and Hills. When Mattathias died, about one year later in 166 BC, his son Judas Maccabee (Hammer) led an army of Jewish dissidents to victory over the Seleucids using guerrilla warfare. Their first target was the many Jews who supported the regime, and pagan altars in Jewish villages were destroyed, boys circumcised, and Jews forced to join their ranks.

Their tactics won out and after defeating the Seleucids, they entered Jerusalem in triumph and ritually cleansed the Temple, re-establishing traditional Jewish worship there and installing Yonatan Maccabee as high priest. Until this day, Jews celebrate the victory over the Seleucids in 166 BC with the festival of Chanukkah, which usually falls around the second half of December.

When the Romans replaced the Seleucids as the region's main imperial force, they granted the Hasmonean king Hyrcanus II (79 BC) limited authority under the Roman governor of Damascus. The Jews were hostile to the new regime, and the following years witnessed frequent insurrections. A final attempt to restore the former glory of the Hasmonean dynasty was made by Mattathias Antigonus, whose defeat and death brought Hasmonean rule to an end (40 BC), and Palestine became a province of the Roman Empire.

In 37 BC, Herod, a son-in-law of Hyrcanus II, was appointed King of Judea by the Romans. He had almost full autonomy in the country's internal affairs, and he launched a massive construction programme. He also remodelled the Temple into one of the most magnificent buildings of its time. But despite his many achievements, he was never trusted by his Jewish subjects.

He died in 4 BC, and ten years later Judea came under direct Roman administration. Growing anger against Roman

suppression of Jewish religious and cultural life resulted in a full-scale revolt in AD 66.

Titus, who led the Roman fight against the Jews of Judea, was the son of the emperor Vespasian (who had commanded the operation in Judea during the first three years of the revolt), and was himself later to become Roman emperor. Titus surrounded the city, and put pressure on the food and water supplies of the inhabitants by allowing pilgrims to enter the city to celebrate Passover, and then refusing to allow them to leave. After Jewish forces killed a number of Roman soldiers, Titus sent Josephus, the Jewish historian, to negotiate with the defenders. Josephus was wounded with an arrow, and the Jews launched another raid on the Romans, almost capturing Titus.

Titus destroyed the city's newly built third wall with a ram, breaching it as well as the second wall, and turned his attention to the area north of the Temple.

But as the fighting was going on – and Josephus's attempts at negotiation were getting nowhere – food, water and other provisions were dwindling inside the city.

Eventually, the Romans gained ground and managed to take the last Jewish outpost near the Temple, the Antonia Fortress. When a Roman soldier threw a burning stick on to one of the Temple's walls, it spread quickly destroying the building. It isn't clear whether the Temple's destruction was one of Titus's goals, since he probably wanted to turn it into a temple to worship Roman gods and dedicate it to the Roman emperor and pantheon.

The Roman legions quickly crushed the remaining Jewish resistance. Some Jews escaped through hidden underground tunnels, while others made a final stand in the Upper City. This defence halted the Roman advance as they had to construct siege towers. The city was completely under Roman control by 7 September and the Romans continued to hunt down the Jews that had fled the city.

Josephus described Titus as moderate. When negotiations failed, witnessed the siege and aftermath. He wrote in *The Jewish Wars*: "Now as soon as the army had no more people to slay or to plunder, because there remained none to be the objects of their fury..., [Titus] Caesar gave orders that they should now demolish the entire city and Temple, but should leave as many of the towers standing as they were of the greatest eminence; that is, Phasaelus, and Hippicus, and Mariamne; and so much of the wall enclosed the city on the west side. This

LEFT *The Destruction of the Temple of Jerusalem,* painted by Francesco Hayez (1791–1882).

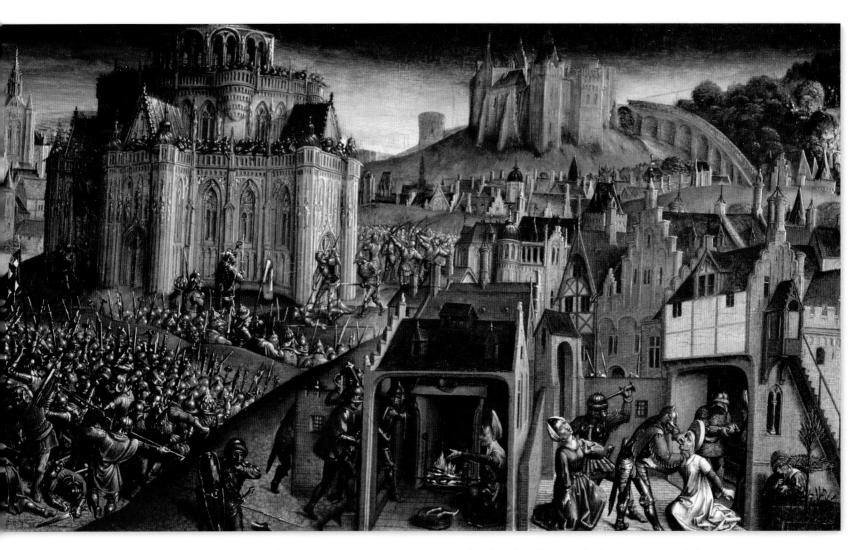

wall was spared, in order to afford a camp for such as were to lie in garrison [in the Upper City], as were the towers [the three forts] also spared, in order to demonstrate to posterity what kind of city it was, and how well fortified, which the Roman valour had subdued; but for all the rest of the wall [surrounding Jerusalem], it was so thoroughly laid even with the ground by those that dug it up to the foundation, that there was left nothing to make those that came thither believe it [Jerusalem] had ever been inhabited...

"And truly, the very view itself was a melancholy thing; for those places which were adorned with trees and pleasant gardens, were now become desolate country every way, and its trees were all cut down. Nor could any foreigner that had formerly seen Judea and the most beautiful suburbs of the city, and now saw it as a desert, but lament and mourn sadly at so great a change..."

Josephus claimed that 1,100,000 people were killed during the siege, of which a majority were Jewish, and that 97,000

were captured and enslaved. Many fled to areas around the Mediterranean. Titus reportedly refused to accept a wreath of victory saying, that the victory did not come through his own efforts but that he had merely served as an instrument of God's wrath.

The destruction of Jerusalem and the Temple was catastrophic for the Jewish people. According to Josephus, hundreds of thousands of Jews perished in the siege of Jerusalem and elsewhere, and many thousands more were sold into slavery.

A last brief period of Jewish sovereignty in ancient times followed Shimon Bar Kokhba's revolt of AD 132, during which Jerusalem and Judea were regained. However, given the overwhelming power of the Romans, the outcome was inevitable. Three years later, in oder to be consistent with Roman tradition, Jerusalem was plowed by oxen, Judea was renamed Palaestinia and Jerusalem, Aelia Capitolina.

Jews would not again control Jerusalem for another 2,000 years, until 1948.

ABOVE *The Taking of Jerusalem by Titus*, Flemish School oil on panel.

OPPOSITE Flavius Josephus (AD 37–c.100), is brought before Titus (AD 39–81) during the siege of Jerusalem (AD 70).

THE SIEGE OF JERUSALEM

In AD 70, the Romans, led by the future emperor Titus, laid siege to Jerusalem. The city had been under the control of Jewish zealots since AD 66 and Titus surrounded the city with four legions. After negotiations failed, Titus started breaching the city walls. As street fighting broke out, he made another unsuccessful bid to negotiate a deal with them. As the fighting intensified and came closer to the Temple, a Roman legionnaire accidently set fire to the building and destroyed it. This was not Titus's goal, as he had wanted to seize the Temple and dedicate it to the Roman emperor and Pantheon.

Jesus of Nazareth and Jerusalem

Jesus, or Yoshua (Joshua) Ben Yosef as he was known at the time, was not born in Jerusalem. According to Christian tradition, his parents travelled from Nazareth in Galilee, 95 kilometres (60 miles) to the north, to Bethlehem, just a few miles south of Jerusalem, where he was born in a cattle shed. The son of a Galilee carpenter, Joseph and his teenage wife Mary (or Mariamme in Aramaic), Jesus visited Jerusalem only a few times – mainly to go to the Temple on Jewish festivals – before his final days in the city, just before the Romans crucified him in around AD 33. The Gospel of Luke describes one of Jesus's visits to Jerusalem as a 12-year-old with his family to celebrate Passover "as usual".

Joseph and Mary were paupers, not much better off than local peasants, but Joseph claimed to be descended from the Davidian line, which, according to Jewish tradition, is where the messiah will come from. During his lifetime, Jerusalem was a great, prosperous and cosmopolitan metropolitan area, and home to the lavishly restored Jewish Temple. Jesus's native Galilee had nothing to compare with Jerusalem. It was one of the biggest cities in the region, with a population of about 80,000 that could more than triple during the Jewish pilgrimages to the Temple at Passover, Tabernacles and Shavuot.

The 12-year-old boy from the sticks would have seen a huge construction site surrounded by a wall up of to 30 metres (100 feet) high. This was not the Temple itself, but the massive platform on which it perched. The city was undergoing a renaissance. Although the Babylonians had destroyed much of Jerusalem's original splendour in 586 BC, on their return from exile 50 years later the Jews had begun rebuilding it. But it was during the rule of Herod the Great, 37–4 BC, that Jerusalem became great again.

Jerusalem was full of wonders, according to Josephus in his *Jewish War*. A case in point is Pontius Pilate's residence, a landmark which was visible to all. It was the place where Pilate condemned Jesus to crucifixion and it was the starting point of his journey to Golgotha, where he met his death and was entombed. However, there is one problem with this: the Church of the Holy Sepulchre, which believers claim marks the spot of the crucifixion, lies within the generally accepted boundaries of the city at Jesus's time, and the Romans as a rule crucified criminals outside the city bounds and did not permit burials within the city walls. A variety of explanations have been suggested, primarily based on changes in the extent of the city at different times.

The stairways to the Temple would, in Jesus's day, have been a bustling cross-section of Jerusalem life, seething with the elite, beggars and the intermingled cries of hawkers, prophets and scholars teaching. It was a small city in itself with thousands of priests and other temple servants, and a massive money-maker that levied huge taxes, and during the festival earned an enormous amount from the animal sacrifices performed there and other offerings.

Archaeological evidence suggests that Jerusalem's elite lived quite well in two-storey houses built around stone-paved inner courts. They had separate baths for regular and ritual cleansing, and the floors boasted fine mosaics; on the walls were frescoes or *trompe l'oeil* stucco that mimicked masonry. Archaeologists have uncovered finely crafted glass goblets and delicate perfume flasks. These of course were elite houses, and Jerusalem had more than its share of the poor and indigent. The "middle class", such as small businessmen, craftsmen and tax collectors, would have been educated at home and at their local synagogue.

The high priest at the time was Caiaphas, an appointee of Valerius Gratus, the Roman procurator who preceded Pontius Pilate, probably through bribery. His job was to defend the Temple, where revolts against foreign rule were usually fomented. Jesus, and others who wanted to be rid of "foreign oppression" and customs, were seen as a threat to the status quo. If it was bad for the Temple, then it would be bad for the Romans and the Jews.

RIGHT According to Jewish tradition, the messiah – the annointed one – would arrive in Jerusalem on a white donkey, as depicted in this fourteenth-century fresco by Italian artist Giotto di Bondone and entitled "Entrance into Jerusalem".

But Jesus had another vision, according to the Gospels. He believed that foreign, non-Jewish control of Jerusalem and the Temple would soon end, precipitating an "End of Days". Although his words, as transmitted – admittedly much later – in the four Gospels spoke of social justice and revolution, his view was a very Jewish one of the days after the end of days. The view put forward in the Beatitudes (Matthew 5: 3–12) "Blessed are the poor, for they shall inherit the Kingdom of Heaven" is a very Jewish view of the messianic era. Jesus didn't invent or found Christianity – he didn't even view himself as the messiah – and nor did his 12 apostles. Christianity came much later, from the writings of Saul – later Paul – of Tarsus, who stepped way beyond the teachings of Jewish law.

His radical preaching drew attention, not least from Herod Antipas, who believed he was the reincarnation of John the Baptist whom he had executed for being a thorn in his side. Herod threatened to arrest Jesus, but the son of Nazareth was forewarned by some of the Pharisees and he escaped Antipas's clutches.

BELOW A nineteenth century French plan for the Church of the Holy Sepulchre, the reported site of Jesus's crucifixion and burial. It was built by Helena, the mother of Byzantine Emperor Constantine in 325–326 CE.

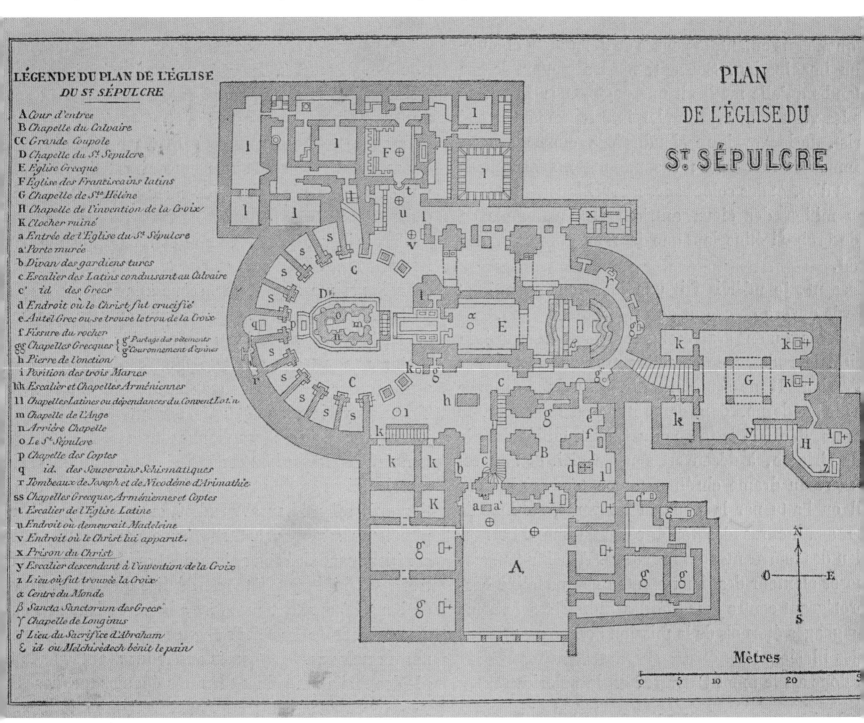

LÉGENDE DU PLAN DE L'ÉGLISE
DU St SÉPULCRE

A Cour d'entrée
B Chapelle du Calvaire
CC Grande Coupole
D Chapelle du St Sépulcre
E Église Grecque
F Église des Franciscains latins
G Chapelle de Ste Hélène
H Chapelle de l'invention de la Croix
K Clocher ruiné
a Entrée de l'Église du St Sépulcre
a' Porte murée
b Divan des gardiens turcs
c Escalier des Latins conduisant au Calvaire
c' id. des Grecs
d Endroit où le Christ fut crucifié
e Autel Grec où se trouve le trou de la Croix
f Fissure du rocher
gg Chapelles Grecques { g' Partage des vêtements
                      { g" Couronnement d'épines
h Pierre de l'onction
i Position des trois Maries
kk Escalier et Chapelles Arméniennes
ll Chapelles Latines ou dépendances du Convent Lot.n
m Chapelle de l'Ange
n Arrière Chapelle
o Le St Sépulcre
p Chapelle des Coptes
q id. des Souverains Schismatiques
r Tombeaux de Joseph et de Nicodéme d'Arimathie
ss Chapelles Grecques, Arméniennes et Coptes
t Escalier de l'Église Latine
u Endroit où demeurait Madeleine
v Endroit où le Christ lui apparut.
x Prison du Christ
y Escalier descendant à l'invention de la Croix
z Lieu où fut trouvée la Croix
α Centre du Monde
β Sancta Sanctorum des Grecs
γ Chapelle de Longinus
δ Lieu du Sacrifice d'Abraham
ε id. où Melchisédech bénit le pain

PLAN
DE L'ÉGLISE DU
St SÉPULCRE

Mètres

0   5   10   20

LEFT *The Crucifixion* by the legendary Flemish old master Peter Paul Rubens.

And despite this warning, Jesus and his supporters entered Jerusalem in a procession in about AD 33 during Passover when the city was at its most crowded. This act of defiance did not, it is safe to say, please Herod or his Roman masters.

Before his crucifixion, Jesus and his disciples held a Last Supper – presumed to be the traditional Jewish Passover meal – in the Cenacle, on the second floor of a building on Mount Zion, said to house the tomb of King David.

On his third day in the city, he was arrested on Herod's instructions with the support of the high priest Caiaphas, and brought before the Roman prefect Pontius Pilate, a hated, bullying figure who liked shows of power.

During his trial, Pilate accused Jesus of being "King of the Jews", a charge Jesus rejected, saying: "Thou sayest thus" (Luke 23:3). This did not impress the prefect who ordered execution by crucifixion, a punishment usually reserved for common criminals. It was a typical Roman punishment as the Jewish leadership, the priests, did not have authority to give death sentences.

Jesus left Jerusalem through the Garden Gate and was taken to Golgotha – the place of the skull – an area of hilly gardens and tombs in rocks that served as the city's place of execution.

After his death, Jesus's followers, who continued to disseminate his message, were really an apocalyptic Jewish sect based in the Temple. Like Jesus, they riled against the authorities who had turned the holy place into a centre of materialism and commerce. During the life of the 12 apostles, these "Jewish Christians" saw their mission as spreading their beliefs among traditional Jewish communities throughout the Roman Empire. Later, through Saul (or Paul) of Tarsus, the word was spread further, so beginning the process by which Christianity ceased to be based in Jerusalem (although always keeping the city at the heart of the faith).

OPPOSITE Jesus drives the moneylenders and merchants from the Temple (John 2:13).

BELOW An oil painting by Martin Feuerstein dating from approximately 1898, showing Jesus falling for the first time, at the third station of the cross on the Via Dolorosa.

JESUS IS CRUCIFIED

Before being crucified, Jesus was treated in the usual brutal manner, facing a whip tipped with metal or bone. This in itself killed many victims before crucifixion. He was also humiliated by being forced to wear a placard saying "Jesus, King of the Jews" that had been prepared by the centurions. He was taken from the Citadel towards the Upper City, and his supporters wept as he walked along what is now the Via Dolorosa, the Street of Tears. He urged them not to cry because, according to the Gospel account, he believed that their lives would be better soon since the messianic era was nigh. Simon of Cyrene urged some supporters to help him with the cross he was bearing.

Jerusalem and Islam

Jerusalem is the third most sacred place in Sunni Islam, after Mecca and Medina. According to Islamic tradition, all previous prophets – particularly Abraham, David, Solomon and Jesus – were associated with the city, and the final prophet Muhammad visited the city on his nocturnal journey on the stallion al-Buraq. For early Muslims, it was the first qibla (direction of prayer) and Muhammad designated the al-Aqsa Mosque for pilgrimage. The seventeenth Sura (chapter) in the Quran states: "Glory to He (God) Who did take His servant for a Journey by night from the Sacred Mosque to the farthest Mosque, whose precincts We did bless." Note that the name of Jerusalem is not mentioned,

which introduces the possibility of different interpretations. In fact, Jerusalem is not mentioned specifically anywhere in the Muslim holy book.

Islam arrived in the Holy Land and Jerusalem towards the end of AD 636, on horseback. The armies of Caliph Omar carried the word of Allah and his prophet Muhammad (who had died in AD 632) out of the Arabian peninsula to the Levant and North Africa (which were then all under Byzantine control).

As the rest of Palestine fell under Muslim control, the remaining Byzantine soldiers concentrated in Jerusalem and tried to hold out there, led by Patriarch Sophronius,

BELOW A nineteenth-century coloured engraving of the entrance of Caliph Omar I into Jerusalem, AD 638. Caliph Omar I was a benevolent leader who allowed Jews and Christians to worship in Jerusalem, and ordered the building of the Dome of the Rock.

a Greek intellectual who had sung the city's praises in his poetry. Jerusalem was, he wrote, "Zion, radiant Zion of the Universe", but his resistance was to no avail.

At the time, the Arab armies – led by Abu Ubaydah ibn al-Jarrah, one of the original ten companions of the Prophet Muhammad – called the city Ilya, after its Roman name Aelia Capitolina, but only later changed it to al-Quds (the Holy Place), which has been the Arabic name for the city ever since.

The siege of the city, in AD 638, lasted for six months, but the Byzantine garrison was so weakened that the patriarch began negotiations to surrender the city. He accepted the payment of a jizya (a poll-tax by paid non-Muslims living in a Muslim-controlled state), as long as Caliph Omar came to Jerusalem to sign the pact and accept the surrender himself.

Although the Muslims tried to trick Sophronius by sending someone posing as the Caliph, the ruse did not work as the stand-in was recognized. When the stratagem failed, Abu Ubaydah wrote to Caliph Omar about the situation, and invited him to come to Jerusalem to accept the surrender of the city.

Omar responded to his commander's plea and in early April of AD 638, Omar went to the Holy Land and Jerusalem and signed a pact known as The Omariyya Convenant by which Sophronius surrendered Jerusalem in exchange for pledges of religious and civil freedom for the Christians (who would, however, have to pay the jizya). In late April the surrender became official and Omar entered Jerusalem, riding side by side with his former adversary Sophronius.

For the first time in almost 500 years, Omar allowed Jews to live in Jerusalem and worship at their holy sites. Muslim chroniclers recorded that at the time of the dawn prayers, Sophronius issued an invitation to the caliph to pray inside the Church of the Holy Sepulchre. Omar, however, turned this down, for fear that his Muslim followers would take this as a pretext to convert the church into a mosque and thus breach the terms of the recently signed Covenant.

The caliph stayed in Jerusalem for ten days, during which time he was taken to Temple Mount and shown the Foundation Stone. According to Muslim tradition, the stone marks the spot where Muhammad ascended heavenwards during his night flight from Mecca, the Isra and Mira'aj. Later Muslim tradition held that Omar himself helped clear the area of refuse and discovered the stone. As a result, he ordered that the area be fenced off and a mosque built nearby. The Gallic bishop Arculf, who lived in Jerusalem at the time, described this mosque as being rectangular and capable of holding 3,000 worshippers. The area was developed further by the Umayyad Caliph Abd al-Malik (AD 685–705) who built the Dome of the Rock on the site in order to compete with the grandeur of nearby churches.

After the Crusades, both Christians and Muslims believed the Dome of the Rock to be part of Solomon's Temple, and the Knights Templar set up their base there. Some of their churches in Europe borrow from its multi-sided design, including the twelfth-century Templar Church in London's Inner Temple – mentioned in Dan Brown's *The Da Vinci Code* – whose round nave is very reminiscent of the mosque.

Near the Dome of the Rock stands the silver-domed al-Aqsa – or Furthest – Mosque, so-called to denote the furthest point Muhammad reached on his night journey on al-Buraq. Capable of holding about 5,000 worshippers at any given time, it is the largest mosque in Jerusalem and its many architectural styles denote the various influences of several of those who have ruled Jerusalem over the centuries.

Muslims today make up almost 30 per cent of the population of Greater Jerusalem, and live mainly in suburbs and villages to the east and north of the city.

There are some families who have been there since the advent of Islam – the Shishaklis, the Husseinis, the Judehs, the Nuseibehs and the Qazaz – who have been Muezzin on Temple Mount for half a millennium.

Because of the political situation between Israel and the Palestinians, there is always tension between Jerusalem's Jews and Muslims. The Muslims feel alienated by the Israeli rule over those parts of the city it captured in the 1967 Six-Day War, which sometimes leads to violence and bloodshed.

BELOW Jerusalem has always benefitted from trade, tourism and merchants, as can be seen in this souq (market) in the Arab Quarter of the Old City, Jerusalem.

OVERLEAF Palestinians at Friday prayers near the Dome of the Rock on the Temple Mount, Jerusalem, 1998.

The Crusades

The Crusades that caused so much death, destruction and hostility between Muslims and Christians were the idea of one man. Pope Urban II made it his life's mission to restore the glory and pre-eminence of the Roman Catholic Church. To do so he had to prevent the Seljuk Turks from making more territorial gains in the crumbling Byzantine Empire, and regain sovereignty of the Holy Land and its centre Jerusalem from the hands of the Saracens.

The idea for the Crusades began at the Council of Piacenza, in March 1095, when Urban received an ambassador from the Byzantine Emperor Alexios I Komnenos (1081–1118). The emperor wanted help against the Muslim Turks, who had taken over most of formerly Byzantine Anatolia. At the Council of Clermont in November, Urban is said to have delivered a sermon ordering people to wrestle the Holy Land and the Eastern churches from the Turks.

LEFT This image, a detail from *Les Passages Fait Outremer (Overseas Voyages)* by Sebastian Mameret, depicts a battle during the First Crusade.

The First Crusade (1096–1099) was an armed pilgrimage. No Crusader could consider his journey complete unless he had prayed at the Church of the Holy Sepulchre.

In Jerusalem, Jews and Muslims fought together against the Crusaders during the Siege of Jerusalem (1099). Outside the walls, the Crusaders were dispirited. It was hot, their water supplies low – many of the wells they controlled had been poisoned – and their horses had died in the heat or had been used as food. But driven by religious fervour, the Crusaders marched around the city, some barefooted, with trumpets and banners. The Crusader armies were far superior in arms, manpower and tactics, so the local inhabitants were without much of a chance. With several siege towers, the Crusaders advanced on the city walls and within hours of bloody fighting the city had fallen. Those who did not flee were massacred, and the Crusaders pillaged or destroyed synagogues, mosques and most of the city.

RIGHT An entrance to the Church of the Holy Sepulchre in Jerusalem, allegedly built in AD 335. The existing church was built in 1810, but the original site is disputed. A few traces of the building erected by Constantine remain, and subsequent churches built over the site were destroyed by the Turks and Tartars.

As the fighting ended and the Crusaders took control of the city, Godfrey was left in control of a city in ruins. He had only 300 knights and 2,000 soldiers, and there were very few surviving citizens.

Towards the end of the year, Godfrey was forced to cede the city to his brother Baldwin, the Count of Edessa, who was working on the Pope's orders to establish a religious kingdom. Baldwin was crowned in the Church of the Nativity in Bethlehem and named King of the Latins in Jerusalem.

On a raid into Egypt, in 1118, Baldwin fell ill and died, and was succeeded by his cousin Baldwin II, named the Small. He gave the Temple Mount over to the Templars, an order known for its chastity, poverty and obedience. They started small – just nine knights to begin with – but they grew into a formidable force of 300 knights.

There now followed a period of relative peace and co-existence in Jerusalem, but after the Muslims conquered the town of Edessa, a new Crusade was urged by Bernard of Clairvaux. French and South German armies marched to Jerusalem in 1147 but failed to make any gains.

Jerusalem in this time grew and played host to soldiers from across western Europe, from Norway in the north to Italy in the south. And they mingled with eastern Christians, Armenians, Georgians, Greeks and Syrians. It also stared to fill up with merchants from Genoa and Venice, and as the number of soldiers grew, so did the number of taverns and amount of prostitutes.

For almost 40 years, Muslim leaders did not counter the religious fervour of the Crusaders with their own. However, in 1137, Zangi, the Muslim ruler of Mosul and Aleppo, sensing a growing fervour in his population, set out to restore Islamic pride.

Against that background, the Muslims started to claw back what had been taken from them almost half a century previously. Out in the east, a new force was rising. The Kurdish warrior king Saladin – or, in Arabic Salah al-Din – had fought off his rivals in what is now Iraq and wanted now to attack the Crusader kingdom.Because of princely rivalries within the Crusader kingdom, Saladin's work was made easier, and on 4 July 1187 the Crusaders were totally obliterated at the Battle of Hattin. In October that year, Saladin captured most of Jerusalem.

The Muslim's capture of Jerusalem led to the Third Crusade (1189–92). King Philip II of France (1179–1223) joined King Richard I (The Lionheart) (1157–99) and Barbarosa, the Holy

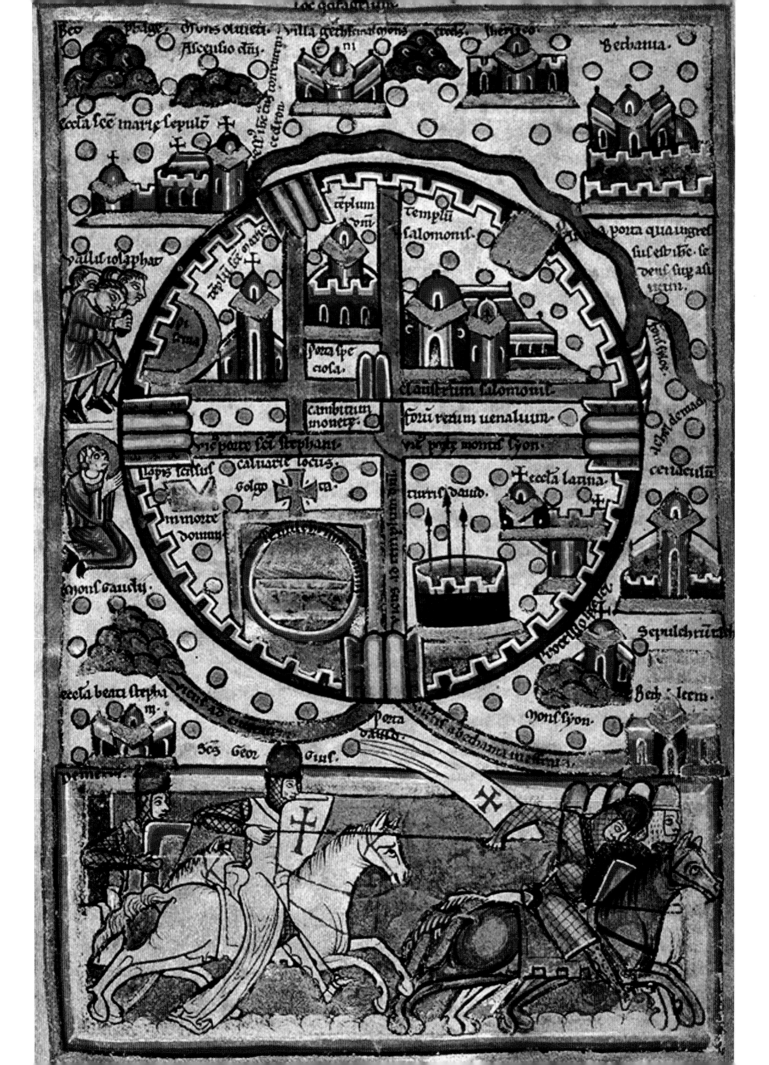

Roman Emperor Frederick I (1122–90). Unfortunately for Barbarosa, he drowned en route and never made it to the Holy Land. While Philip and Richard initially travelled together, the British and French armies split in Lyons with Richard deciding to go by sea and Philip overland. They rejoined in Messina and marched on the Holy Land and to take part in the siege of Acre. After Acre fell, on 12 June 1189, Philip became ill with dysentery and lost his will to fight. He also resented the way Richard claimed that he and he alone had taken Acre and decided to return to France.

When Richard I arrived in the Holy Land in 1191, he defeated Saladin at the Battle of Arsuf, and at the Battle of Jaffa in 1192, recovering most of the coast, but could not recover Jerusalem or any of the inland territory of the kingdom. Conrad of Montferrat, a northern Italian, was named de facto king of Jerusalem through his marriage to Isabella of Jerusalem in 1190, and was officially elected monarch in 1192 – just days before his death. Following his death, Isabella, now heavily pregnant, married Count Henry II of Champagne, a nephew and close associate of Richard I.

The Crusade ended peacefully in 1192, with the Treaty of Ramla. Saladin allowed pilgrimages to be made to Jerusalem for prayers at Christian holy sites, after which most of the Crusaders returned home. Those Crusaders who remained in the Holy Land rebuilt their kingdom, creating several small Crusader states including the Kingdom of Jerusalem where 120,000 French-speaking Western Christians, the Franks, ruled over 350,000 Muslims, Jews, and native Eastern Christians who had remained since Muslim rule began in AD 638.

Until the mid-1200s, there were a few more Crusades as Christian Europe sought to take advantage of disunity among Muslims after the death of Saladin. In the Fifth Crusade of 1215, Austrian and Hungarian armies joined the King of Jerusalem and the Prince of Antioch to take back Jerusalem, where they faced the Sultan al-Kamil. In the Sixth Crusade, 1228–29, there were no battles as Frederick II made peace with al-Kamil. In Kamil, Frederick found a kindred spirit, as both were interested in philosophy and the arts. The treaty allowed Christians to rule over most of Jerusalem and a strip of territory from Acre to Jerusalem, while the Muslims were given control of the Dome of the Rock and the al-Aqsa Mosque. Nowadays, some people talk about this as a blueprint for a deal between Israel and a future Palestinian state.

In 1225, Frederick married Yolanda, the heiress to the kingdom of Jerusalem, and when she died three years later, he crowned himself King of Jerusalem. Peace lasted for about a decade, but as the Muslims were not happy that al-Kamil had relinquished control of Jerusalem, they besieged it until 1244, when they regained control of the city.

OPPOSITE The Crusaders sought to gain control over the holy sites, Jewish, Christian and Muslim, throughout the Middle East. This twelfth-century map of Jerusalem and Palestine includes the sacred sites and the Temple of Solomon.

BELOW This fifteenth century illuminated manuscript from The Chronicle of David Aubert depicts Balian of Ibelin surrendering and handing over the keys to the Tower of David.

SALADIN

A Kurdish Muslim, Salah ad-din Yusuf ibn Ayyub (1138–1193), was the first Sultan of Egypt and Syria and the founder of the Ayyubid dynasty. Renowned for his sense of chivalry, justice and fairness, he was a formidable fighter as his success at the Battle of Hattin showed. A strict adherent to Sunni Islam, he became a renowned figure. At its fullest, his sultanate encompassed Egypt, Syria, Mesopotamia, Hejaz and Yemen. A clever and well-educated man, he worked his way up through the ranks of the armies of Imad ad-din Zengi, eventually becoming regent of Aleppo and the leader of the Zengids. He established the Abbasid caliphate in Egypt in 1171 and went on to make many conquests from that base. He captured Jerusalem in 1187 and retained it despite the efforts of the Third Crusade. Although he and King Richard the Lionheart agreed a treaty, with Richard's sister being given in marriage to Saladin's brother, the two men never met. Saladin died of a fever in March 1193, not long after Richard left the Holy Land.

The Church of the Holy Sepulchre

Down the labyrinthine alleyways of Jerusalem's Old City, on the site that Christians venerate as Golgotha (the Hill of Calvary) – where Jesus was supposedly crucified and buried – stands the Church of the Holy Sepulchre, which the Eastern Orthodox Churches also call the Church of the Resurrection. The church is home to the Stone of Anointing, which Christians believe is where Jesus's body was prepared for burial by Joseph of Arimathea. The tradition only seems to have arisen since the Crusades, and the current stone has only been in place since 1810.

Christians have made pilgrimages to the church since at least the fourth century AD. Today it serves as the headquarters of the Greek Orthodox Patriarchate of Jerusalem. The building is under the control of a number of rival Christian groups, in centuries-old arrangements as labyrinthine as the nearby alleyways.

This division of responsibility has meant that no one Christian group is allowed to control the building, and times and places of worship for each community are strictly regulated in common areas. In fact, ultimate control of the building is out of Christian hands altogether. In 1192, the legendary leader of the Saracens Saladin gave control of the main gate of the building to the Muslim Nuseibeh family.

Today, the church is home to Eastern and Oriental Orthodox (such as Coptic Orthodox) groups as well as Roman Catholics – all of them considered to be the original churches. Post-Reformation Churches, such as the Anglicans and the Lutherans, have no permanent presence there.

The site has always been a place of worship, but not always a church. In the early second century AD, the site served as a temple of Aphrodite. In the fourth century, Constantine, the first Christian Roman emperor, ordered the demolition of the temple, directing his mother Helena to build a church there. In about AD 325, she went to Jerusalem to oversee the construction, even reportedly involving herself in the work and allegedly discovering the "True Cross" – on which Jesus was said to have been crucified. The anniversary of the consecration of the church is celebrated by Eastern Orthodoxy on 13 September (according to the Julian calendar), which is 26 September according to the West's Gregorian calendar.

The building was damaged by fire and the "True Cross" captured and taken in AD 614, when Jerusalem was conquered by the Persians. It was returned in AD 629 by Emperor Heraclius (AD 610–41) as part of the peace treaty that ended the Persian-Byzantine War.

Since Muslims view Jesus as one of the prophets of Islam, the early Muslim rulers protected the city's Christian sites, and prevented their destruction and use as houses. But towards the end of the tenth century, the Holy Sepulchre church's doors and roof were burnt during a riot.

LEFT Constantine, the Holy Roman emperor who converted his empire to Christianity, and his mother Helena with the alleged "True Cross" that she found. A 1502 painting by Cima da Conegliano, which is now housed in the church of St Giovanni in Bragora, Venice, Italy.

Muslim protection of the church was not indefinite. In 1009, the Fatimid Caliph al-Hakim bin-Amr Allah (996–1021), angered by the scale of the Easter pilgrimage to Jerusalem, ordered the church's total destruction. The Christian writer Yahya ibn Sa'id reported that everything was razed "except those parts which were impossible to destroy or would have been too difficult to carry away". The Church's foundations were hacked down to bedrock.

The reaction in Europe was furious, with many rulers blaming the Jews, who were expelled from several French towns. However, in 1027–28, an agreement was reached under which al-Hakim's son and heir Ali az-Zahir agreed to the rebuilding and redecoration of the church. This work was finally completed in 1048 by Emperor Constantine IX Momomachos and Patriarch Nicephorus of Constantinople. In return, they allowed a mosque to be re-opened in the Byzantine capital, where sermons praised az-Zahir.

In addition the Byzantines, while releasing 5,000 Muslim prisoners, made demands for the restoration of other churches destroyed by Al-Hakim and the re-establishment of a

Patriarchate in Jerusalem. Despite the Byzantines' expenditure of vast sums on the project, a total replacement was far beyond the available resources, so the new construction was concentrated on the rotunda and its surrounding buildings.

As the balance of power between various Muslim rulers shifted, control of Jerusalem alternated several times between the Fatimids (based in Egypt) and the Seljuks loyal to the rival Abbasid caliphate in Baghdad.

During the twelfth century the church was renovated again, as recorded by the chronicler William of Tyre. During the building work, the Crusaders found part of the original ground level of Hadrian's temple and decided to create a chapel dedicated to Helena, excavating a staircase to reach it. The church was refurbished in a Romanesque style and a bell tower added. These renovations unified the small chapels on the site and by 1149, during the reign of Queen Melisende, all the holy places were finally united under one roof and the church became the seat of the Latin Patriarchs.

Although the church was lost to Muslim control after Saladin's conquest in 1187, the terms of the treaty after the

ABOVE Pilgrims in front of the Church of the Holy Sepulchre from the *Livre des Merveilles de Monde* (*Book of the Marvels of the World*), by the French illuminator Boucicaut Master and his workshop. This book is commonly referred to as The Travels of Marco Polo and is a collection of stories about his voyages, as told by Polo and collected by Rustichello da Pisa.

Third Crusade permitted Christian pilgrims to continue to visit it. The church, in common with the rest of the city, briefly came back under Christian control in 1229 when it was regained by Emperor Frederick II, but it was lost again in 1244 after Jerusalem's sack by the Khwarezmians.

Franciscan friars further renovated the Holy Sepulchre in 1555, as it had been neglected despite increased numbers of pilgrims. After this, control of the church changed hands several times between the Franciscans and the Orthodox Christians, depending on which community could obtain a favourable order from the Ottoman authorities at any given time. Bribery and violent clashes were not uncommon.

The structure was severely damaged by a fire in 1808, which caused the dome of the Rotunda to collapse, smashing the exterior decoration. The Rotunda and exterior of the Edicule (the church's shrine) were rebuilt in 1809–10 in Baroque style.

Another *firman* (decree of the Ottoman sultan), in 1853, solidified the existing territorial division among the communities and set an arrangement to "remain forever", causing almost insoluble differences of opinion about upkeep and even minor changes, including disagreement on the removal of an exterior ladder under one of the windows. It's still there, more than 150 years on.

Even after the 1853 settlement, the church was afflicted by periodic outbreaks of violence. In the summer of 2002, the action of a Coptic monk in moving his chair from the spot which the agreements allowed into the shade led to attacks on the Copts by the Ethiopians, and a brawl in which 11 were injured. In 2004, the Franciscan chapel's door was left ajar during the Orthodox celebration of the Exaltation of the Holy Cross. This was seen as an affront by the Orthodox group and another fight broke out, leading to several arrests. Violence flared once more on Palm Sunday 2008, after the expulsion of a Greek monk from the building by members of another sect. The police who came to his rescue were attacked by an enraged mob.

RIGHT The Miracle of the Holy Fire in the Church of the Holy Sepulchre during the Christian Orthodox Easter. Thousands of Orthodox Christians celebrate Easter here.

Mamluk Rule

With the failure of the Crusaders to regain any foothold in Jerusalem after their loss of the city in 1244, it came under the rule of the Mamluks from 1260 to 1516.

The Mamluks were initially the bodyguards of the Ayyubid sultans of Egypt (Saladin's successors). As they were born outside Egypt – in what is now the southern Caucasus in Russia – and were infants when bought as slaves, they owed allegiance to no one but the sultan and became his elite military force.

After the death of Sultan as-Salih Ayyub in 1249, the Mamluks became so powerful that they seized control of his domains (including Jerusalem) in 1260. They formed themselves into a formidable ruling warrior class that held power for 250 years until their defeat and the conquest by the Ottoman empire in 1516. They also moved their centre of rule from Cairo to Damascus.

As far as the Mamluks were concerned, while Jerusalem held great religious significance for the three monotheistic faiths – and they catered for pilgrimages for Jews, Christians and Muslims, seen as a huge tax revenue source (since at times the pilgrims doubled Jerusalem's population) – the city itself was strategically, politically and economically of only peripheral interest to them.

The city's governance was left in the hands of the clerics, whose job it was to maintain religious sites. The general population lived in abject poverty, with most of the city's residents earning their livelihood by providing services to pilgrims or working in the cotton industry.

While much of the city was neglected, the period witnessed construction on religious sites on a massive and grandiose scale. The buildings on Temple Mount were renovated, with arches being erected around the Dome of the Rock. Bathing and drinking facilities were also added to the Mount, improving the facilities for pilgrims immeasurably. The Mamluks also placed some new government buildings there, built bridges to the Mount and renovated the streets around it in the Old City, including the Chain Street and Cotton Makers' Street, as well as Lions' Gate. On these streets they built hostels and soup kitchens for the pilgrims and outside the city walls they built retreats for priests. They also restored the markets and hostels for Christian pilgrims.

But Jerusalem was also a place of exile and punishment for officers and officials who had fallen foul of the Mamluk authorities. These exiles – from all over the Mamluk empire – contributed their talent to the building and day-to-day running of the city, and acted to some extent as a civil counterbalance to the predominantly clerical governance of the city.

With the exception of raids by Mongols in 1299, the first raids of Peter, King of Cyprus from 1365 to 1369, and a brief Tartar invasion in 1401, Jerusalem enjoyed a period of relative peace under early Mamluk rule. But despite the best efforts of the exiles and the clerics, Jerusalem was a city in decline and decay, especially after the mid-fifteenth century,

when a series of raids by Bedouin tribesmen left the city's water supply destroyed. As a result, those not connected religiously to the city abandoned it.

The Jewish population of the city grew during the Mamluk period, from two families to several hundred by the early sixteenth century. Although most of the Jews were of Spanish Sephardi origin, some were Ashkenazis – northern Europeans, mainly from Warsaw. Their numbers were bolstered during the three Jewish pilgrimages, Passover (Pesach), Tabernacles (Succot) and the Feast of Weeks (Shavuot). The highlights for these Jewish pilgrims were visits to the Western Wall, the Mount of Olives and Mount Zion. The Mamluks cleaned

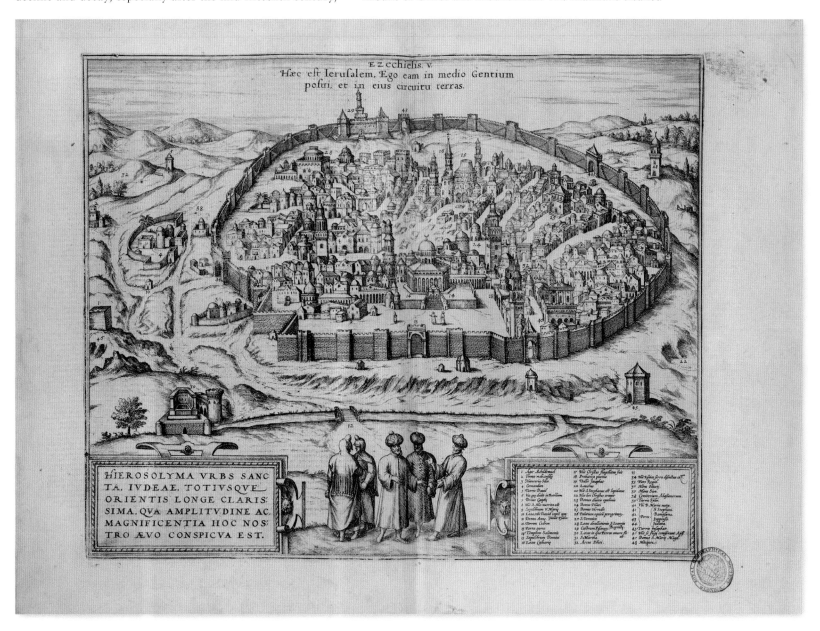

OPPOSITE A view of the city of Jerusalem by Burchard du Mont Sion, c.1455. From *Advis directif pour faire le passaige d'outre mer* (*Advice for People Travelling Overseas*).

ABOVE Throughout the ages, several maps of the Holy City have been created, showing its development over the centuries. This one, from 1572, is by Georg Braun, the topo-geographer who edited the *Civitas Orbis Terrarum*.

the areas adjacent to the Wall, allowing access to the Wall itself. However, construction of bridges, buildings and streets elsewhere in this area sometimes caused blockages, so the Jews had to pray elsewhere.

Among the Jewish visitors in the late thirteenth century was Rabbi Moses Ben-Nachman, also known as Nachmanides. He was a prolific scholar, who, as well as being a rabbi, was a philosopher and physician, and produced commentaries on the Bible. Fleeing persecution in Spain, he sought refuge in Jerusalem, which he made his home in 1267, aged 72. There he set about establishing Jewish institutions, including an Old City synagogue that still exists today. He encouraged the development within the city of a new Jewish community – which had faded away during Crusader times – and this marked the beginning of an uninterrupted Jewish presence in Jerusalem.

ABOVE Selim the Grim (1512–1520), the ninth sultan of the Ottoman Empire, entered Jerusalem in 1517, and despite his nickname allowed Jews and Christians freedom of worship.

RIGHT Marco Polo before Kublai Khan. A miniature painting from John Mandeville's *The Book of Marvels and Travels.* Kublai Khan asked Marco Polo in 1266 to bring him consecrated oil from Jerusalem but Polo was delayed in doing this. In 1271 he eventually set off to fulfill Khan's wish, returning to him with the oil in 1275.

There were conflicts between the Jews and the Christians over some sites, especially Mount Zion, which the former saw as the place of King David's burial and the latter considered to be the location of the Last Supper. In the end, the Mamluks intervened and prevented the Christians from holding prayers there, which in turn caused problems for the Jews back in Europe.

The era saw the start of the first printed travel guides and the canon of Mainz Cathedral Bernhard von Breydenbach wrote the *Peregrinatio in Terram Sanctam* (*Journey in the Holy Land*) in 1486. The *Peregrinatio* was the first illustrated travel book to be printed, and it included a map of Palestine and the first folding pages to appear in printed form. Von Breydenbach's companion Erhard Reuwich illustrated the book and he is the first such illustrator to be named in print.

LEFT Marco Polo sailing from Venice in 1271. With his father and uncle Polo (1254–1324) left Venice to fulfill a promise to Kublai Khan. This image is from a late-fifteenth-century illuminated manuscript.

RIGHT The Black Death, which spread over Europe and the Near East from Asia, hit pilgrimages and commerce in Jerusalem. This 1866 engraving "The Plague of Jerusalem" was done by French printmaker Gustave Doré in 1866.

THE BLACK DEATH

Another visitor to Jerusalem – this time unwanted – was the Black Death, which swept through the Holy Land in the mid-fourteenth century on its way from Asia to Europe. The pestilence reached the Holy Land by way of Egypt and Gaza, whence it spread up the coast and inland to Ashkelon, Acre, Jerusalem, Damascus, Homs and Aleppo. In Jerusalem, the Black Death caused huge disruption to religious and commercial life because it curtailed pilgrimages, leading to a huge knock-on effect on commerce and income.

Rebirth and Re-establishment

wing to the major influx of Jews from Europe and the creation of neighbourhoods outside the Old City's walls, in the nineteenth century Jerusalem started its transformation from a religious backwater to an urban centre. At the start of the century, there were about 9,000 inhabitants. By 1900, the population had reached 55,000, almost two-thirds of it Jewish.

The city's development was also influenced by competition between European powers; France backed the Catholics, Prussia and England established Protestant bishoprics and the Russian tsar extended his protection to the Greek Orthodox community.

Contact with the European imperial powers began at the end of the eighteenth century when Napoleon tried to conquer

the area to prevent British access to their territories in India through the Levant. Facing him was the commander of the Ottoman forces in Palestine Ahmet Jazzar Pasha. Napoleon had not reckoned on Jazzar's ability to get British help, and Commodore Sir William Sidney Smith helped repel three Napoleonic assaults on Acre. On 21 May 1799, Napoleon was forced to withdraw. Back in Egypt, he realized the magnitude of his defeat and left for France, never to return to the region.

Napoleon's misadventure in the Middle East sparked a renewed European interest in the area, with Jerusalem being accorded mythological status. One of the main promoters of this view was the French traveller François-René, vicomte de Chateaubriand, who described Jerusalem as a "deicidal city" filled with "heap loads of rubbish" in his 1811 book *Itinéraire*

de Paris à Jérusalem (*Itinerary from Paris to Jerusalem*).

In 1831, Benjamin Disraeli visited Jerusalem and he, too, was shocked at city's state. He viewed the Jews and Arabs as the same, and castigated the Christians for not believing in Judaism. Twenty years later, he recalled his visit and said that restoring the Jewish people to their land, which could be purchased from the Ottomans, was not only possible, but right.

But the Ottomans were not that keen on selling Palestine or Jerusalem to Britain, especially not under its new ruler, the official in charge of Egypt, Mehmet Ali. One of his devices for gaining control of the Ottoman provinces was through his ruthless son Ibrahim "the Red". When, in 1833, Mehmet Ali conquered the Levant and was poised to capture Constantinople, the Ottoman sultanate did a deal with him,

ABOVE In this painting by W Heath entitled "The Siege of Saint Jean D'Acre", the Turks, supported by a force of seamen under Sir Sidney Smith, resist Napoleon's attempts to take the town, even when the walls were breached on 8 May 1799.

73

whereby he would rule Egypt, Arabia and Crete and Ibrahim would govern Greater Syria.

In government, Ibrahim instituted reforms in Jerusalem, allowing Christians and Jews far more freedom of worship and promised them equality under the law. However, any revolt – and there were several – was not tolerated. As uprisings grew in frequency, Ibrahim became more ruthless, beheading anyone opposed to him.

In 1839, Ibrahim made a move on Constantinople and gained French support for his effort. However, the British sided with the Ottoman. This prevented Ibrahim from moving on Istanbul, but the young Sultan Abdulmecid had to issue a ruling allowing equality for religious minorities. Ibrahim invited the Europeans to open consulates in Jerusalem, and Britain's first vice-consul William Turner Young embarked on a mission to convert Jews to Christianity to hasten the Second Coming.

Another believer in the imminence of the Second Coming was the US consul-general to Syria Warder Cresson, who arrived in Jerusalem in October 1844. Cresson, who had sampled practically every cult going, had been persuaded by a rabbi in Pennsylvania that salvation would come only when the Jews returned to Zion. By the time the US government realized that they had appointed a madman, Cresson was already in Jerusalem, issuing visas for Jews.

The Russians too were trying to stake a claim on Palestine. The Russian Orthodox Church was heavily involved in Jerusalem. Nicholas I, who became Tsar in 1825, was part of a tradition that believed that every Russian should make a pilgrimage there. These pilgrimages worried the British, who saw them as a pretext for a Russian takeover. They suspected too that increasing French interest in the religious life of the city also had a political motive.

NAPOLEON AND JERUSALEM

As Napoleon was leading his forces from Jaffa – the port closest to Jerusalem – to the old Crusader port of Acre in the north, one of his commanders General François-Étienne de Damas, requested permission to conquer Jerusalem. Napoleon denied the request, saying that he himself would lead the attack on the city – once he had conquered Acre – so he could "plant the tree of liberty in the ground where Jesus suffered". Napoleon also made promises to the Jews, whom he described as "the rightful heirs of Palestine" in a proclamation of 20 April 1799. In a declaration that pre-dates Zionism by almost a century, Bonaparte proclaimed: "Arise then, with gladness, ye exiled! A war... waged in self-defence by a nation whose hereditary lands were regarded by its enemies as plunder to be divided... avenges its own shame and the shame of the remotest nations..."

BELOW Napoleon Bonaparte never made it to Jerusalem – he made the mistake of first wanting to conquer the coastal plain, but faced stiff resistance from the Ottomans backed up by the British. In this painting by Antoine Jean Gros the French are victorious over the Turks at the Battle of Nazareth, 8 April 1799.

The Dome of the Rock

The Dome of the Rock is located at the centre of Temple Mount – in Arabic Haram al-Sharif (the Noble Sanctuary) in the Old City of Jerusalem. It was built on the instructions of the Umayyad Chaliph Abd al-Malik in AD 691 and has been refurbished many times since.

The rock after which it is named is known as the Foundation Stone. According to Islamic belief, it is the site of the Isra and Mira'aj, the two parts of the Night Journey that the Prophet Muhammad took during a single night around the year AD 621. In the journey, Muhammad travels on the steed al-Buraq to "the farthest mosque" (al-Aqsa) where he leads other prophets in prayer. He then ascends to heaven where he speaks to God, who gives Muhammad instructions to take back to the faithful on Earth about the number of times to offer prayers each day.

The two engineers in charge of the project are given as Yazid Ibn Salam from Jerusalem and Raja Ibn Haywah from Baysan. Muslim sources say that Caliph Abd al-Malik hoped that it would "house the Muslims from cold and heat", and intended the building to serve as a shrine for pilgrims and not as a mosque for public worship.

Indeed it doesn't look like a mosque commonly used for public worship. Its rotunda roof looks like an attempt to rival the many Christian domes of its time, shaped as it is like a Byzantine martyrium. A C Cresswell, in his book *Origin of the Plan of the Dome of the Rock*, notes that those who built the shrine used the measurements of the nearby Church of the Holy Sepulchre.

The building is in the shape of an octagon and has a 20-metre (66-foot) diameter wooden dome mounted on an elevated drum consisting of a circle of 16 piers and columns. Surrounding this circle is an octagonal arcade of 24 piers and columns. The porcelain outer side walls each measure approximately 18 metres (59 feet) wide and 11 metres (36 feet) high. Both the dome and the exterior walls contain many windows.

The interior of the dome is decorated with mosaic and marble, much of which was added several centuries after its completion. It also contains Quranic inscriptions. These clearly display a spirit of polemic against Christianity, while stressing that Jesus was a true prophet. The formula "*la sharika lahu*" (meaning "*God has no companion*") is repeated five

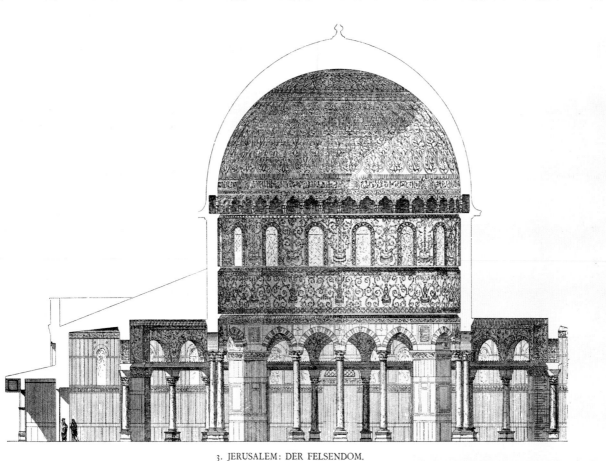

3. JERUSALEM: DER FELSENDOM.

times and verses 19:35–7 from Sura Maryam, which strongly reaffirm Jesus' prophethood to God, are quoted together with the prayer: "*Allahumma salli ala rasulika wa'abdika Isa bin Maryam*" – "*In the name of the One God [Allah] Pray for your Prophet and Servant Jesus son of Mary*".

During the time of the Crusader Kingdom, the Dome of the Rock was given to the Augustinians, who turned it into a church while the al-Aqsa Mosque became a royal stable. The Knights Templar, who believed the Dome of the Rock was the site of the Temple of Solomon, later set up their headquarters in the al-Aqsa Mosque adjacent to the Dome for much of the twelfth century. They called it the *Templum Domini* and it featured on the official seals of the Order's Grand Masters. It became the architectural model for Templar churches across Europe.

When the city was recaptured for the Muslims by Saladin, in October 1187, the Noble Sanctuary was reconsecrated for Islam. The cross on top of the Dome was replaced by a golden crescent, and a wooden screen was placed around the rock below. Then, during the Mamluk period (1250–1510), the sanctuary was the focus of extensive sultanic patronage.

When the Ottoman Turks conquered the land and during the reign of Suleiman the Magnificent (1520–66), in a seven-year project, the exterior of the Dome of the Rock was covered with Iznik tiles, highly decorated ceramics from the Turkish town of Iznik that were produced between the late fifteenth and seventeenth centuries.

Adjacent to the Dome of the Rock, the Ottomans built the free-standing Dome of the Prophet in 1620. During the reign of Ottoman Sultan Mahmud II, large-scale renovation was undertaken in 1817. However, many of the repairs that had taken place over previous years were rendered useless when the Dome of the Rock was badly shaken during an earthquake in Palestine on 11 July 1927.

In 1965, the Dome was covered with a durable aluminum and bronze alloy made in Italy, which replaced the lead exterior. In 1993 – when the building was under Israeli control – the golden dome covering was refurbished following a donation of $8.2 million by King Hussein of Jordan who sold one of his houses in London to fund the 80 kilograms (176 pounds) of gold required.

Israel took control of the Dome of the Rock during its victory in the Six-Day War in 1967. A few hours after the Israeli flag was hoisted over the Dome in 1967, the then Defence Minister Moshe Dayan ordered its removal and gave the Muslim *waqf* (religious trust) the authority to manage the Temple Mount, in order to "keep the peace". The Dome is now maintained by the Ministry of Awqaf in Amman, Jordan.

Until the mid-nineteenth century, non-Muslims were not permitted in the area. Since 1967, non-Muslims have been given limited access, however they are not allowed to pray on the Temple Mount, or to carry any form of religious artefact or anything with Hebrew letters. The Israeli police help enforce this. They are, however, still prohibited from entering the mosques and accessing the Temple Mount through the Cotton Market.

A number of buildings have been designed as copies of the Dome of the Rock. These include the octagonal Church of St Giacomo in Italy, and the octagonal Moorish Revival-style Rumbach Street synagogue in Budapest. This was done because the Dome of the Rock was long believed by Christians to echo the architecture of Solomon's Temple in Jerusalem, as can be seen in Raphael's *The Marriage of the Virgin* (1504) and in Perugino's *Marriage of the Virgin* (1500–04).

RIGHT The lavish interior of the Dome, which has been rebuilt several times in its long history.

Outside the City Walls

At the beginning of the eighteenth century, there were about 1,200 Jews living in Jerusalem – the vast majority of whom were Sephardi, or Jews of Spanish or Turkish origin.

However, at about the same time, the city became a magnet for other Jews who wanted to make the Land of Israel their home. In 1700, about 1,500 Ashkenazi – northern European – Jews set out from Shedlitz in Poland for Jerusalem after hearing the words of the itinerant rabbi Yehdud He'Chasid who wanted Jews to redeem the Holy Land for Judaism. Unfortunately, many died on the long and arduous trek and the rabbi passed away a few days after arriving in Jerusalem.

These were the first of a series of ultra-Orthodox Jews who left their European homes during the eighteenth and nineteenth centuries to make a new home in the Holy Land, and especially in Jerusalem. A few rebuilt the ruins of the Hurvat Yehudah He-Hasid Synagogue and, in 1830, about 20 disciples of Rabbi Moshe Sofer, the Chasam Sofer – one of the greatest rabbinical authorities – moved to Holy Land and set up home in Jerusalem.

A need to build outside the Old City walls was exacerbated in 1837 when an earthquake destroyed many Jewish settlements in Galilee, including the holy towns of Safed and Tiberius, and the residents had to find alternative accommodation in Jerusalem.

RIGHT The Moses
Montefiore windmill
in the Yemin Moshe
area of Jerusalem. The
British philanthropist
Montefiore wanted
the Jews of Jerusalem
to stop relying on
handouts, so he built
them a windmill in a bid
to get them to work.

OVERLEAF The Yemin
Moshe section of
Jerusalem.

LEFT In recent years Jerusalem has become a world-renowned centre of arts and culture. Nassim Daqwar plays the violin and Tiasar Alias the lute for Ethnic Music Week at the Jerusalem Music Centre in March 1999. The Jerusalem Music Centre is located in Mishkenot Sha'ananim

The greatest supporters of the move outside the walls – where there was little work and great danger from marauding Bedouin Arab tribes – was Sir Moses Montefiore, a nineteenth-century banker, philanthropist and a Sheriff of the City of London. Sir Moses visited Jerusalem for the first time in 1827 – an event which he later claimed changed his life – followed by several more visits in 1838, 1849, 1855, 1857, 1866 and 1875. He made his last trip at the age of 91.

After his first visit, Montefiore became more religiously observant, regularly attending synagogue services. He was the executor of the will of his friend the American philanthropist-businessman Judah Touro, who died having bequeathed money to fund Jewish residential settlements in Palestine.

With the money Montefiore built the alms-houses of Mishkenot Sha'ananim (Peaceful habitation) – a name taken from the Book of Isaiah 32:18: "My people will abide in peaceful habitation, in secure dwellings and in quiet resting places". This was the first neighbourhood outside the walls. These alms-houses are in an area called Yemin Moshe, which is named after Montefiore. Because of the Bedouin raids, the Jews were fearful of moving there, despite comparatively luxurious accommodation (compared to the dereliction of the Old City, that is).

First established in 1860, with two rows of two-bedroom apartments, Sir Moses paid people to live there and the compound was fenced and gated. Residents had to abide by a set of strict rules, including having daily to recite prayers for Touro.

Montefiore also created work for them by building a windmill which was designed as a flour mill. Apart from providing employment, it was established to wean the residents off charities from abroad, which was their main income. Unfortunately, the windmill never really became operable, but today a group of Dutch Christian supporters of Israel are trying to have it renovated for its original purpose. Nowadays, the windmill serves as a small museum dedicated to Sir Moses's achievements.

Today, Mishkenot Sha'ananim has been turned into an upscale guesthouse that is frequented by internationally acclaimed authors, artists and musicians visiting Israel. It also houses the Jerusalem Music Centre and the Jerusalem Centre for Ethics. A second row of houses was built in 1866 to accommodate people who were fleeing a cholera epidemic in the Old City.

Later, Montefiore established the two Knesset Yisrael neighbourhoods, one for Sephardi Jews, and the other for Ashkenazim, which were even further away from the city walls than Yemin Moshe. He also built a printing press and textile factory, and helped to finance several agricultural colonies outside Jerusalem. He was unable to secure agricultural land,

MOSES MONTEFIORE

Sir Moses Haim Montefiore, First Baronet, Kt (1784–1885) was born in Italy but grew up in London. He retired in 1824 to devote his time and money to philanthropic work, travelling to places such as Rome, Russia, Morocco and Romania. He was knighted by Queen Victoria in 1837, and in 1846 was given a baronetcy for his services on behalf of Jewish humanitarian causes.

however, because the Ottoman authorities placed severe restrictions on its sale to non-Muslims.

Another neighbourhood outside the walls is the ultra-Orthodox Meah She'arim, today one of the most colourful in Jerusalem. A visit there is like stepping back to the eighteenth century and the residents do not take kindly to people, especially women, they consider being dressed "immodestly". It was established in 1874 by 100 shareholders as the second settlement outside the walls. It was intended to rehouse people suffering from poor sanitation in the Old City.

Given its no-nonsense, isolationist ultra-Orthodox nature it is ironic that its architect was Conrad Schick, a German Christian missionary. The building work was organized by Joseph Rivlin, a leading figure in Jerusalem's Jewish community, and a Christian Arab from Bethlehem.

The quarter had the first street light in Jerusalem. It was surrounded by walls and had gates that were locked at night to prevent raids by nearby tribes. Twenty years later, the quarter had grown three-fold and it had a flour mill and a bakery. A planned open green space in each courtyard was never accomplished, but cowsheds were built instead.

Zion and the Dawn of a New Era

The founder of modern political Zionism, the Austrian-Hungarian journalist and literary critic Theodor Herzl, was a totally assimilated Jew. He did not circumcise his son and had Christmas trees at home. But he was shocked to the core by reports of anti-Semitic pogroms in Russia in 1881, and when an anti-Semite Karl Lueger was elected mayor of his hometown Vienna in 1895, he wrote of a "mood of despair" among the city's many Jews.

In 1894, he was sent to Paris to cover the trial of Alfred Dreyfus, a French Jewish army officer who was accused of spying for Germany. The trial was a set-up, and Herzl was shocked even further to see the crowd baying for Dreyfus's blood, chanting "*Mort aux Juifs*" ("Death to Jews"). Happening, as this was, in a country that had granted Jews emancipation, Herzl came to the conclusion that assimilation had failed abysmally and would lead to even greater anti-Semitism.

He had a vision for a Jewish state, a predominantly secular one, where citizens would play tennis and cricket. He set this all out in his 1896 book *The Jewish State* where he proclaimed: "Palestine is our ever-memorable historic home... The Maccabees will rise again. We shall live as free men on our own soil and die peacefully in our own homes."

A Jewish yearning for Zion was not new: Jews prayed towards Zion, they wished each other "Next Year in Jerusalem" at the end of the Passover meal, and some made pilgrimages there three times a year. Herzl just gave this yearning a name, Zionism, and a political expression.

Political Zionism appeared at a time of rising European race-based nationalism, where the Jews did not fit in. Already back in 1862, Moses Hess, an early comrade of Karl Marx, wrote in his *Rome and Jerusalem* – an early proto-Zionist tract – that this nationalism would spawn anti-Semitism.

In August 1897, Herzl chaired the First Zionist Congress in Basel, Switzerland, where he declared: "In Basel, I founded the Jewish state. If I said this out loud today, I would be greeted by universal laughter. Perhaps in five years, certainly in 50, everyone will know it." He was not far wrong. Israel was established in May 1948, 55 years after Herzl's declaration.

Herzl, however, believed he needed the backing of a great imperial power, and because he believed the Jewish state should be German-speaking (as was he), he approached the German Kaiser Wilhelm II. Coincidentally, the Kaiser was

ABOVE The Austrian journalist and assimilated Jew Theodor Herzl in Altaussee, August 1900. Shocked by the anti-Semitism at the trial of Alfred Dreyfus in France, Herzl decided that the Jews needed self-determination and created political Zionism.

OPPOSITE The front page from *Le Petit Journal* covering the trial of Alfred Dreyfus. This image shows his swored being broken and all signs of his military rank being removed as part of his disgrace and punishment.

planning a trip to the Middle East where he would meet his ally, the Ottoman Sultan Abdulhamid II. He would then travel on to Jerusalem to dedicate The Church of the Redeemer close to the Church of the Holy Sepulchre, on land that had been given to his father, Frederick.

Herzl met the Kaiser in Istanbul, just before the meeting with the Sultan in 1898. The Kaiser agreed to support the plan, mainly because he believed the "usurers" (the Jews) would be better employed working with their hands than relying on on hand-outs from philanthropists and religious institutions abroad and from income derived from Jewish pilgrims as they had before. Montefiore wanted the Jews of the city to be industrious and to earn money from labour. The Kaiser presented the case to the sultan, who rejected it out of hand saying: "The Jews may spare their millions. When my empire is divided, they may get Palestine for free. But only our corpse can be divided."

The Kaiser agreed to another meeting with Herzl in Jerusalem itself, which the Kaiser entered, like a messiah, on a white horse. Herzl and Kaiser Wilhelm met again in Palestine on 29 October 1898, at Mikveh Israel, an agricultural school near present-day Holon, Israel. This meeting signified the first time that the Zionist movement, headed by Herzl, had sought support from a European imperial power.

Herzl had another, more formal, public audience with the Kaiser at the latter's tent camp – which was described as the "largest party in Jerusalem since the Crusades" – on the Street of the Prophets in Jerusalem, on 2 November.

Neither the Kaiser nor Herzl liked Jerusalem. Wilhelm described it as a "dismal arid heap of stones spoilt by large suburbs of Jewish colonies where 60,000 of these people are living, greasy and squalid, cringing and abject, doing nothing but trying to fleece the neighbours…"

Herzl said that "if Jerusalem is ever ours, I will clean up everything not sacred, tear down the filthy rat holes… I'd build an airy, comfortable, properly sewered brand new city around the holy places", envisaging a Jewish Lourdes. In fact, he said Jerusalem should not belong to any one country or religion, it should be extra-territorial.

Herzl also believed that all that was necessary for a Jewish state were 300,000 Jews. Meanwhile, Jewish predominance in the city – out of a population of 45,500, the Jews numbered 28,000 – was beginning to worry local Arab leaders.

A pogrom in Kishinev, in 1903, sparked an anti-Semitic killing spree across Russia, resulting in many Jews fleeing to Palestine (as well as the United States and Britain). One Arab leader Yusuf Khalidi wrote to his friend the Chief Rabbi of France Zadok Kahn that while the Jews had historical rights to Jerusalem, the reality was that a return would result in a bloody clash with the native Arabs. And how right he was.

OPPOSITE The programme of the first Zionist Conference in Basel, Switzerland. "Were I to sum up the Basel Congress in a word – which I shall guard against pronouncing publicly – it would be this: At Basle I founded the Jewish State."

TRANSLATION:

Zionism strives for the establishment of a publicly and legally secured home in Palestine for the Jewish people.

For the attainment of this aim the Congress plans the following means:

1. Appropriate promotion of the settlement of Palestine with Jewish farmers, artisans and tradesmen.

2. The organization and gathering of all Jews through suitable local and general institutions, in accordance with the laws of the various countries.

3. The promotion of Jewish national sentiment and consciousness.

4. Preparatory steps for the attainment of such Government consent as is necessary in order to achieve the aim of Zionism.

OVERLEAF Jewish refugees arrive in Israel waving the future flag of the State of Israel. The flag, with its Star of David was designed for the Zionist Movement in 1891.

Programm.

Der Zionismus erstrebt für das jüdische Volk die Schaffung einer rechtlich gesicherten Heimstätte in Palästina.

Zur Errichung dieses Zieles nimmt der Congress folgende Mittel in Aussicht:

I. Die zweckdienliche Förderung der Besiedlung Palästinas mit jüdischen Ackerbauern, Handwerkern und Gewerbetreibenden.

II. Die Gliederung und Zusammenfassung der gesamten Judenschaft durch geeignete örtliche und allgemeine Veranstaltungen nach den Landesgesetzen.

III. Die Stärkung des jüdischen Volksgefühls und Volksbewußtseins.

IV. Vorbereitende Schritte zur Erlangung der Regierungszustimmung, die nötig sind, um das Ziel des Zionismus zu erreichen.

DAVID BEN-GURION

David Ben-Gurion (1886–1973) has the distinction of being the founder and the first prime minister of Israel. As prime minister (1955–63), he was keen to develop the country and also encouraged Jewish immigration to Israel. Ben-Gurion worked closely with the German government to ensure reparations for Germany's treatment of Jewish people during the Second World War. He left politics altogether in 1970.

BELOW Israel's first prime minister David Ben-Gurion. He believed that the State of Israel had to be established even though it did not include the whole of Jerusalem.

The First World War

On the eve of the First World War, Jerusalem was in ferment. There were masses of Jews entering Palestine and Jerusalem, encouraged by Zionist leaders who beseeched them to build "Jewish towns, particularly in Jerusalem", and driven by the rise of anti-Semitism in Eastern and Central Europe.

As Jews had already purchased the land on which the Hebrew University would be built on Mount Scopus, there was alarm among Jerusalem's Arabs. However, despite their concerns, several well known landowning families, such as the Husseinis, sold land to the Zionists. In the Arabic-speaking parts of the city, there was an increase in nationalism, sparked by the realization that the area's Ottoman Turkish rulers, for all their talk of reform, were no less venal and corrupt than those who had gone before them. In fact, these "Young Turks"

– members of the ultra-nationalist Committee of Union and Progress who wanted to reform the absolute monarchy of the sultanate – were proving to be more brutal than their predecessors. They suppressed any rise in Arab national consciousness – through the Jaffa-based *Filastin* nationalist newspaper – and prevented even the study of Arabic.

Yet what scared the Arab nationalists most was the rise of the Zionists. In the Istanbul parliament, French-educated deputy speaker Ruhi Khalidi, a scion of an old Jerusalem family, tried to pass a law banning the sale of land to Jews. Another candidate for the parliament, Ragheb al-Nashashibi, from another old Jerusalem family, said he would dedicate "all his energies to removing the danger of Zionism".

When the war broke out, in August 1914, the Turks, then run by the "Three Pashas" – ultra-nationalists who believed in the "Turkicization" of the empire to stop it being "the sick man of Europe" – sided with the Germans. Sultan Mehmet V Raschid declared war on Britain, France and Russia on 11 November and a jihad (holy struggle) was proclaimed at the al-Aqsa Mosque. At first, even Jerusalem's Jews supported the Turks and they welcomed the German commander Baron Friedrich Kress von Kressenstein to the city. He and his forces gave protection to the Jews from the British.

A week after the war broke out, one of the Three Pashas Ahmet Jemal, by then Minister of the Marine, became effective dictator of Jerusalem and Greater Syria. One of his German officers Franz von Papen described this poker-playing playboy as "an extremely intelligent Oriental despot". He ruled with an iron rod: "I make the laws and unmake them," he said as he terrorized Jerusalem, especially the Arab nationalists of whom he and the other Ottoman leaders were suspicious; he either had them executed or sent into Anatolian exile.

However, being a despot and playboy did not make Jemal an accomplished military commander, and an attempt in February 1915 to invade British-held Egypt failed miserably. Jemal blamed his failures on "Arab spies" working for the British and started a killing spree in Jerusalem that saw hundreds if not thousands hanged at the Jaffa and Damascus gates. Although he also suspected the Jews of helping the British too, their leader David Ben-Gurion (who was later to become Israel's first prime minister) recruited for the Ottoman forces.

LEFT Sultan Mehmet V (1844–1918), the last of the Ottoman leaders, oversaw the collapse of the "sick man of Europe" when he sided with the Germans during the First World War.

OPPOSITE David Ben-Gurion as a young soldier in the Jewish Legion, part of the British Army, in 1918.

LEFT Hussein al-Husseini, the mayor of Jerusalem (shown third from right), surrenders the Jerusalem to Sergeant F H Hurcomb (shown fifth from right).

OPPOSITE After Allenby's entrance into Jerusalem, Haddad Bey reads Allenby's official proclamation of martial law in the city.

Jemal tried also to charm the Jews and Arabs into reconciliation, hosting meetings between Ben-Gurion and the Husseinis with a view to setting up a joint Arab-Jewish homeland under Turkish auspices. When that failed to work, he expelled 500 Jews and banned Zionist symbols, prompting anger in Germany and Austria. This annoyed Jemal even further, and he threatened to treat the Jews as the Ottomans had dealt with the Armenians: "I will execute anyone who lays a finger on a single orange. If you want peace and quiet, the Berlin and Vienna press must be quiet," he said.

But Jemal was not above doing deals. He tried to court Jewish support for the Turkish war effort, offering the Jewish Henry Morgenthau, the American ambassador to Istanbul, the chance to buy the Western Wall. He repeated the offer to Jerusalem's Jews, whose number had dropped by 20,000 through illness and starvation.

While the city was rotting away, Jemal conducted a debauched life-style, with orgies and massive banquets for his German and Turkish officers. He claimed to marry Leah Tennenbaum, a glamorous Jerusalem socialite (whose house in the Talpiot neighbourhood later hosted the exiled Ethiopian Emperor Haile Selassie and was owned by Israeli military leader and politician Moshe Dayan).

As Jemal was living a life of debauchery and terrorism in Jerusalem, the Arabs were indeed plotting with the British against the Ottoman Empire. Talks between T E Lawrence ("Lawrence of Arabia") and Sherif Hussein, the ruler of the Arab Hejaz, led to the outbreak of the Arab Revolt in 1916. Lawrence was working for two British officials, Sir Henry McMahon, the high commissioner in Egypt, and Sir Mark Sykes, an MP and diplomatic adviser, on a plan to entice the Arabs into rising up against the Ottoman empire.

The British agreed that Hussein should have a kingdom, but not comprising the whole of the Levant and Arabia as he had demanded, because the British Empire had its own interests there.

Another problem was that France, Britain's ally in the war, also had interests in Palestine which had to be taken into account. Unknown to Hussein, Sykes and his French counterpart, François Georges-Picot, who had served in Beirut, agreed to carve up the Middle East for the post-war era, with France getting Syria and Lebanon, and Britain taking control of Iraq and some of Palestine. There would also be an Arab kingdom – under British supervision – and Jerusalem would be internationalized under French, British and Russian control.

In June 1916, Hussein launched the Arab Revolt and declared himself King of all Arabs, later downgraded to King of Hejaz on the insistence of Britain. Hussein's revolt succeeded in the Hejaz and the area that is today Jordan, but failed beyond there. As all this was happening, the British were massing forces in Egypt under Field Marshal Edmund Allenby, 1st Viscount Allenby. He had been appointed to lead the Egyptian Expeditionary Force, whose mission was to spearhead the British attack on Palestine and Syria in 1917–18.

Lawrence thought highly of Allenby: "[He was] physically large and confident, and morally so great that the comprehension of our littleness came slow to him." The force pushed northwards towards Jerusalem after battles in Gaza and Beersheba, and captured the city on 9 December 1917.

In the surrender text, the city's mayor Hussein al-Husseini wrote: "Due to the severity of the siege of the city and the suffering that this peaceful country has endured from your heavy guns; and for fear that these deadly bombs will hit the holy places, we are forced to hand over to you the city through Hussein al-Husseini, the mayor of Jerusalem, hoping that you will protect Jerusalem the way we have protected it for more than five hundred years."

On 11 December, General Allenby entered the Old City on foot through the Jaffa Gate. As a mark of respect, he left his horses and vehicles behind. Allenby was the first Christian since the Crusades to control Jerusalem.

He stated in his official report: "I entered the city officially at noon, 11 December, with a few of my staff, the commanders of the French and Italian detachments, the heads of the political missions, and the Military Attaches of France, Italy, and America... The procession was all afoot, and at Jaffa Gate I was received by the guards representing England, Scotland, Ireland, Wales, Australia, New Zealand, India, France and Italy. The population received me well."

British prime minister David Lloyd George described Jerusalem's capture as "a Christmas present for the British people". And Allenby is said to have remarked: "The Crusades have now ended." But the war against the West – and the Zionists – was only just beginning.

OPPOSITE British troops in Jerusalem waiting for General Allenby in January 1918 following their occupation of the city.

The al-Aqsa Mosque

The al-Aqsa Mosque, the silver-domed building on Temple Mount, is the third-holiest site in Sunni Islam. In Arabic, al-Aqsa means "the furthest" – and it is considered the furthest point the Prophet Muhammad reached on his night journey on his steed al-Buraq from Mecca to Heaven (the Isra and Miraj).

With its beams made from Lebanon cedarwood and local cypress, the al-Aqsa mosque sits on an artificial platform that Herod's engineers constructed to help alleviate problems caused by the topography of the mount. The mosque compound has an area of 140,000 square metres (1,507,000 square feet), with the area of the building itself 35,000 square metres (368,000 square feet). It can hold up to 5,000 worshippers and is about 80 metres (260 feet) long and 55 metres (18 feet) wide.

For almost one and a half years after his migration from Mecca to Medina (the *hegira* in Arabic) in AD 622, Muhammad and his followers prayed, like the Jews, towards the Temple Mount. It was only after the Jews rejected the prophet's teachings that the Muslims – and Muhammad – began to pray instead toward the giant black Ka'aba stone in Mecca.

Guy le Strange, in *Palestine Under the Moslems* (1980), writes that the mosque was built with materials salvaged from the destroyed Church of Our Lady (which lay on the current site of the al-Aqsa mosque). Through the ages the mosque has undergone various renovations and improvements, with the addition of a dome, minarets and an imam's pulpit.

In the seventh century, the walls of the 112-x-39-metre (367-x-128-foot) mosque were renovated by Caliph Omar. The building underwent a further major restructuring at the time

LEFT Tiles from the mosque's interior – Islamic tile designs often feature script. In other parts of the mosque, there are complex geometric patterns, typical of the beautiful Islamic tile-work that has evolved as a result of the prohibition on depicting human beings or animals.

OPPOSITE The exterior of the al-Aqsa Mosque, the third-holiest place in the Sunni Muslim world).

Ezechielis V.

Hæc est Ierusalem. Ego eam in medio Gentium posui, et in eius circuitu terras.

HIEROSOLYMA VRBS SANC
TA, IVDEAE, TOTIVSQVE
ORIENTIS LONGE CLARIS
SIMA, QVA AMPLITVDINE AC
MAGNIFICENTIA HOC NOS
TRO ÆVO CONSPICVA EST.

of the Umayyad Caliph Abd al-Malik (AD 685–705), which included the adding of a basement, the building of gates and the construction of the Dome of the Rock. It was not, however, until the time of Abd al-Malik's son al-Walid I (AD 705–15) that this work was completed.

Jerusalem was hit by a series of earthquakes during AD 713–14 and the eastern section of the mosque was destroyed. Abd al-Walid, the caliph at the time, ordered its rebuilding, with finance coming from the gold in the Dome of the Rock which was melted down and made into coins. Another severe earthquake in AD 747 caused further damage and necessitated additional major repairs and renovations, and this time the Abbasid Caliph melted down the gold and silver plaques on

the mosque gate to pay for the rebuilding.

In AD 780, his successor, Muhammad al-Mahdi (AD 775–85), rebuilt the mosque, shortening and narrowing the building. The renovation was recorded by the tenth-century Jerusalem-born geographer al-Muqadassi, who wrote that it had "fifteen naves and fifteen gates".

During the Crusades, the mosque was used as a stable. And when Saladin conquered the city from the Crusaders in 1187, he ordered that the building be repaired in double-quick time to prepare it for Friday prayers. Toilets and grain stores put in by the Crusaders were removed, the floors were re-carpeted and its interior was perfumed with rosewater and incense. However, the Ottomans – who captured Jerusalem in

ABOVE An illustration to commemorate wall constructed around the city by Sultan Suleiman the Magnificent, who did much to improve the living conditions in Jerusalem and protect the city against marauders. The illustration used Georg Braun's map as its basis.

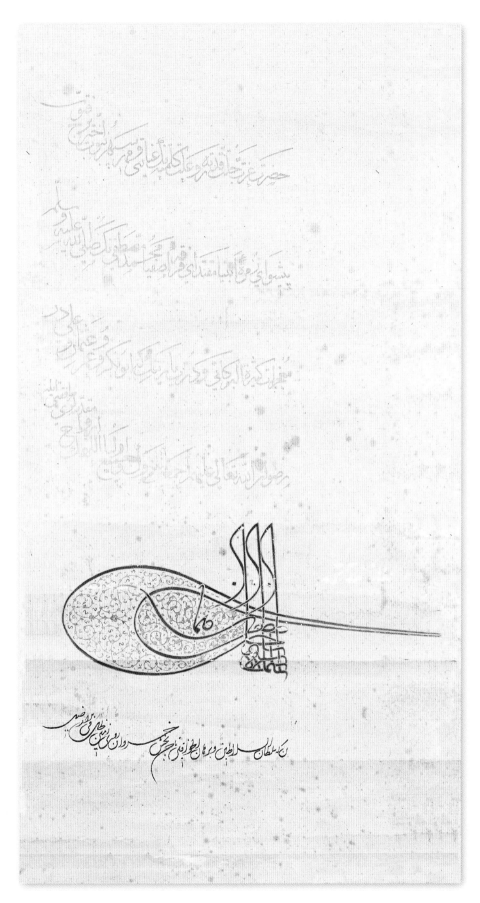

ABOVE A letter by Sultan Suleiman the Magnificent regarding the building of a mosque in Jerusalem from September 1528.

1517 – had little time for the building and any work on the mosque was done at the behest of the local governor, not the sultanate in Istanbul.

When Ottoman Sultan Selim the Grim arrived in the city to take control, he prostrated himself near the mosque, exclaiming: "I am the possessor of the first qibla." Despite his grim name, he confirmed that Jews and Christians would be allowed freedom of worship on Temple Mount.

His son Suleiman succeeded Selim when he died in 1520. Suleiman described a dream where had been visited by the Prophet Muhammed who told him to redecorate and embellish al-Aqsa in order to prevent the infidels taking over.

In 1553, Suleiman wanted to visit Jerusalem and inspect his achievements as the self-proclaimed "Second Solomon and King of the World". Unfortunately for him, however, he never made it because he became embroiled in wars.

His work on the mosque – the dome alone needed more than 40,000 tiles, which were manufactured in a factory set up right next to the building – created a major influx of residents and money as the city's population tripled in size to 16,000.

In the twentieth century, renovations were undertaken in 1922 by the British-appointed Grand Mufti of Jerusalem Haj Amin al-Husseini. He commissioned a Turkish architect to restore the building, including reinforcing the ancient foundations, cleaning and straightening interior columns, replacing wooden beams and replacing the wood in the central area with concrete. In 1927 and 1937, two further earthquakes hit the region, once again causing severe damage to the Mosque.

Even more damage was done to the mosque on 21 August 1969, when an Australian Christian fundamentalist named Denis Michael Rohan set fire to it, hoping to spark a holy war. The fire destroyed the *minbar* (pulpit) installed by Saladin. Rohan, who was afterwards incarcerated in a mental hospital, had imagined that the destruction of the al-Aqsa would usher in the second coming of Jesus and the restoration of the Jewish Temple.

RIGHT Firefighters work to get the blaze on the roof of the al-Aqsa Mosque under control on 21 August 1969. The fire had been started by a mentally unstable Australian Christian who wanted to start a holy war and bring about Armageddon.

107

The British Mandate

The end of the First World War left the Middle East in a chaotic and unstable situation. The defeat and collapse of the Ottoman Empire had been followed by the carving up of the region between France and Britain, accompanied by a series of a contradictory promises to Arab and Jewish nationalists.

Officially, Palestine was under British rule, in a form known as the British Mandate for Palestine, a legally constituted commission to govern the area that was formally confirmed by the League of Nations on 24 July 1922 and which came into effect on 26 September 1923.

The Mandate formally established British rule in the southern regions of former Ottoman Syria and lasted from 1923 to 1948. Britain split the Mandate territory into two administrative regions: Palestine was under direct British rule, while Transjordan came under the rule of the Hashemite family from Hejaz (now Saudi Arabia).

Under the terms of the Mandate – which was to allow the mandated power to administer parts of the Ottoman Empire "until such time as they are able to stand alone" – the powers (most notably Britain and France) accepted the November 1917 Balfour Declaration from the British government to Lord Rothschild that it viewed "with favour the establishment in Palestine of a national home for the Jewish people ... it being clearly understood that nothing shall be done which might prejudice the civil and religious rights of existing non-Jewish communities in Palestine, or the rights and political status enjoyed by Jews in any other country".

ABOVE A coach arrives in Hebron to salvage possessions from Jewish homes after a disturbance, c.1930. More than 65 Jews were murdered in the 1929 Hebron massacre and instances of violence took place many years afterwards.

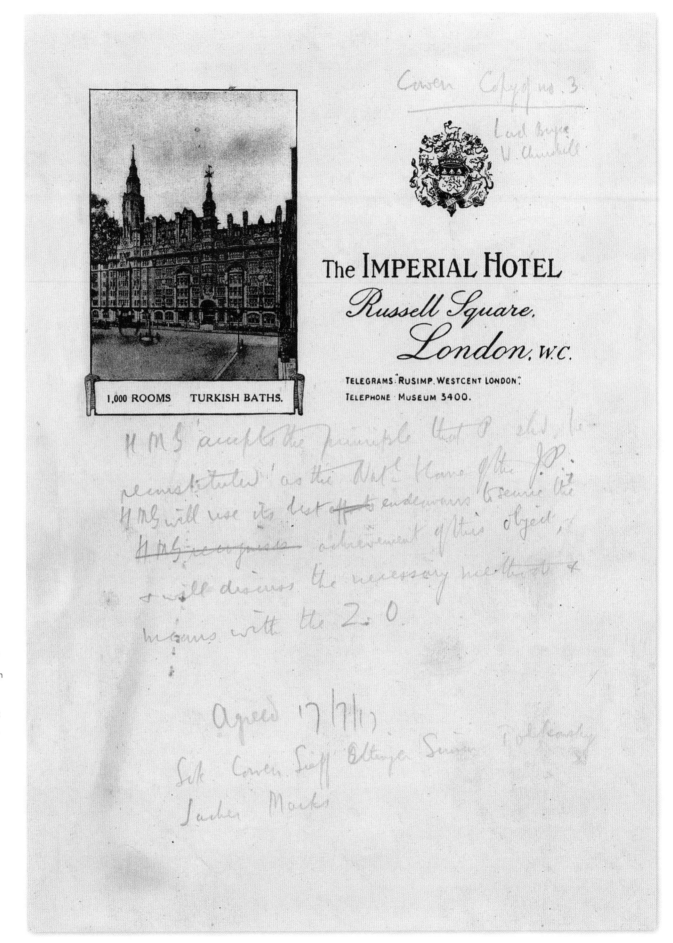

RIGHT A handwritten draft of the
1917 Balfour Declaration written
by Foreign Secretary Lord Balfour
to Lord Rothschild. The declaration
says: "His Majesty's government
view with favour the establishment
in Palestine of a national home for
the Jewish people, and will use
their best endeavours to facilitate
the achievement of this object,
it being clearly understood that
nothing shall be done which may
prejudice the civil and religious
rights of existing non-Jewish
communities in Palestine, or the
rights and political status enjoyed
by Jews in any other country."

Balfour had form with the Zionists. He had offered Uganda as a national homeland of the Jews in 1903 and in 1906 he met Chaim Weizmann, the leader of the Zionist movement.

Weizmann tried to persuade this old Etonian son of Scottish and English aristocracy that millions of Jews wanted a return to Zion, to Jerusalem. However, Balfour responded that the Jews he knew – the Anglo-Jewish leadership who derided Zionism as an Eastern European fetish – didn't want anything to do with Weizmann and his colleagues. Weizmann retorted: "But you meet the wrong kind of Jews."

After much to-ing and fro-ing between the British, French, the Arab nationalists under Hussein, and the Jewish nationalists under Weizmann and David Ben-Gurion, it was decided that Britain would administer the 23 per cent of the area of the Mandate of Palestine west of the River Jordan as "Palestine", while the 77 per cent east of the Jordan would be "Transjordan". As the Mandate came into effect, there were debates among the Zionists and the British over what exactly "a national home for the Jewish people" meant. Some among the Zionists, especially the General Secretary of the Zionist Organization Nahum Sokolow, contended that it was not a fully fledged Jewish state. "The 'Jewish State'," he wrote in his *History of Zionism* "was never part of the Zionist programme. The Jewish State was the title of Herzl's first pamphlet, which had the supreme merit of forcing people to think. This pamphlet was followed by the first Zionist Congress, which accepted the Basel programme – the only programme in existence."

By June 1922, the British were already seeking ways to backtrack on the Balfour Declaration. The Colonial Office sought to restrict Jewish nationalism so that it would not create "the disappearance or subordination of the Arabic

ABOVE The French delegation to the third general assembly of the League of Nations pose for a picture in the gardens of the French consulate in Geneva in 1922.

NCE DE LA PAIX   PARIS, LE   31   Octobre 1919

SECRÉTARIAT
DE LA
DÉLÉGATION DU HEDJAZ
•••

Monsieur le Docteur S. Levin.
du Comité de l'organisation sioniste.
LONDRES.

Monsieur.

Je regrette de ne pouvoir assister à la cérémonie de la commémoration du second anniversaire de la déclaration Balfour à laquelle vous avez bien voulu m'inviter.

Je suis cependant très heureux de saisir cette occasion pour vous réitérer mes vœux les plus sincères de voir nos deux peuples travaillant ensemble pour un idéal commun qui est la résurrection de l'Orient.

Nous avons été unis dans le malheur et nous comptons rester unis dans cette nouvelle ère de progrès et de civilisation qui s'ouvre devant nous.

Notre pays libre et indépendant aura beaucou à gagner de la collaboration de nos deux peuples frères, qu'une histoire commune unit si étroitement.

L'évolution de la race juive sémite ne peut être que saluer avec sympathie par les Arabe sémites.

L'Orient a une grande mission a rempli et s'est à nos deux peuples que cette grande tâche incombe, aussi je crois interpréter me sentiments et ceux du peuple Arabe en rendan hommage à la sincérité des chefs sionistes qui travaillent à l'union de nos deux peuple

Veuillez agréer, Monsieur, l'expressi de ma haute considération.

" Signé " Faisal

ABOVE A letter in French by Amir Faisal in October 1919 talking about co-operation between the Jews and Arabs over Palestine. Faisal was in favour of a Jewish homeland in Palestine, as long as it would remain under Arab sovereignty.

TRANSLATION:

31 October 1919

Dr S Levin, the Committee of the Zionist Organization

Sir.

I regret that I am not able to help you with the ceremony for the commemoration of the second anniversary of the Balfour Declaration which you invited me to.

I am very happy to take this opportunity to reiterate my sincere wish to see our two people work together for the common ideal that is the resurrection of the east.

We have been united in our misfortune and we count on remaining united during this new era of progress and civilisation which has opened between us.

Our countries, free and independent, will have much to gain from a collaboration between our two peoples, a common history unites us closely.

The evolution of the Jewish race cannot be greeted with sympathy by the Arab people.

The east is a big mission to be completed and is a great responsibility for our two peoples. I and the Arab people offer respect to the sincerity of the heads of Zionism who work towards a union between our peoples.

I would like you to accept the expression, Sir, of my highest regards.

Faisal I of Iraq

Amir Faisal was king of the Arab Kingdom of Syria for 136 days in 1920 and the King of the Kingdom of Iraq from 1921–33. Faisal attended the Paris Peace Conference in 1919 as leader of the Arab delegation and argued that an independent Arab emirates should be established in the area that had belonged to the Ottoman Empire. On 3 January 1919 Faisal met Chaim Weizmann, President of the World Zionist Organization and signed the Faisal-Weizmann Agreement for Arab-Jewish cooperation. As part of this Agreement, he conditionally accepted the Balfour Declaration with its promise of a homeland for the Jewish people in Palestine. Sadly, this spirit of cooperation was not last and the Arabs refused to accept the U.N's partition plan for Jewish and Arab states in Palestine and eventually attacked Israel.

population, language or customs in Palestine", or "the imposition of Jewish nationality upon the inhabitants of Palestine as a whole".

The Colonial Office also made it clear that, contrary to what the Jews had been led to believe, their national home would not be in the whole of Mandatory Palestine, but in yet to be determined parts of it. Until the start of the Second World War, this issue poisoned ties between the British and the Jewish and Arab populations of Palestine.

In 1937, the British set up a royal commission, headed by Lord Peel, to look into ways of resolving the issue once and for all. He proposed that two states, one Jewish, the other Arab, be set up in Mandatory Palestine. Both the Jewish and Arab leaderships rejected this plan, although Emir – later King – Abdullah of Transjordan urged both sides to accept it. However, the unofficial leader of the Arabs in Palestine, the Mufti Haj Amin al-Husseini, refused even to discuss the issue.

Under the terms of the 1920 San Remo Conference, the rights of the non-Jewish communities in Palestine would be safeguarded, including a prohibition against discrimination in civil and political matters. The Arab leadership repeatedly pressed the British to grant them national and political rights, such as representative government, in preference to Jewish national and political rights in the remaining 23 per cent of the Mandate of Palestine which the British had set aside for a Jewish homeland. Britain, however, made acceptance of the terms of the Mandate a precondition for any change in the constitutional position of the Arabs.

During the Mandate, the Yishuv or Jewish community in Palestine, grew from one-sixth to almost one-third of the population. According to official records, 367,845 Jews and 33,304 non-Jews emigrated to Palestine between 1920 and 1945. A further 50,000–60,000 Jews entered the country illegally during this period as a result of continued persecution in Europe and elsewhere. As Arab resentment and anger grew over the increased Jewish immigration, the British government placed controversial limitations on it. The Jews felt that these quotas were too harsh, while the Arabs said they did not go far enough.

During the time of the British Mandate, both the Jewish and non-Jewish economies grew substantially, with the Jewish sectors increasing 13.2 per cent per annum, while the Arabs grew by 6.5 per cent annually. The salaries grew too, but the Jews' increased more rapidly than their non-Jewish neighbours' did – by more than 2.5 times, in fact.

In the 25 years of British rule, the Jews also managed

to set up the framework of self-rule, with an assembly of representatives, a government in waiting (The Jewish National Council) and a trade union – the Histadrut. They also had a centralized school system.

Higher education was blooming too, with the establishment in 1912 of the Technion University in Haifa, with its emphasis on natural sciences, engineering and architecture, and in 1925 of the Hebrew University on Mount Scopus in Jerusalem. The Hebrew University was established with money from Jewish intellectuals

OPPOSITE British
soldiers search for
survivors in the debris
of the King David
Hotel in Jerusalem, the
British headquarters,
after a bomb explosion
in 1946 that marked
the beginning of the
end of the British
Mandate. The bombing
was carried out by
the paramilitary group
Irgun, led by future
Israeli prime minister
Menachem Begin.

RIGHT The tower of
Jerusalem's YMCA,
can clearly be seen in
the background of this
photograph from 1900.

113

מדינת ישראל

משרד ראש-הממשלה

מדור התעודות

The Historical Connection of the
Jewish People with Jerusalem
Submitted to the Palestine
Partition Commission
by the Jewish Agency

שנת 1.7.1938

המספר 912/8/31

THE HISTORICAL CONNECTION

of the

JEWISH PEOPLE WITH JERUSALEM

Submitted to the

PALESTINE PARTITION COMMISSION

by the

JEWISH AGENCY FOR PALESTINE

***

Jerusalem
July 1st, 1938.

ABOVE AND RIGHT A report entitled "The Historical Connection of the Jewish People with Jerusalem", which was submitted to the Palestine Partition Committee by the Jewish Agency" in 1938 as part of the process that led to the end of the British Mandate in 1948 and the establishment of the state of Israel.

INTRODUCTION

In the historical consciousness of the Jewish people Jerusalem occupies a unique position. Rome was to the Italians the emblem of their supreme achievement in military conquest and political organisation. Athens embodied to the Greeks the noblest that the genius of their people had wrought in the realms of art and thought. The significance of Jerusalem to the Jews is both of the temporal and spiritual order. It is to them the centre of the ancient wordly glory of Israel, the capital of David and Solomon, 'beautiful in elevation, the joy of the whole earth, the city of the great king'. (Psalm XLVIII). Its conquest and elevation to the capital of Judaea by David signified the establishment of a Jewish polity in Palestine. Conversely, its destruction first by the Chaldeans and subsequently by the Romans, marked in each case the end of Jewish statehood. On its recapture the last efforts of the nation were spent in the abortive revolt of Bar Cochba half a century after the Roman conquest. In each of these wars Jerusalem was defended with desperate tenacity. It was never surrendered, but only reduced after a fierce struggle. And as soon as the pressure of the conqueror relaxed Jewish settlement was resumed. As will be shown in the present survey, an almost unbroken chain of Jewish settlement connects present-day Jerusalem with the holy city of antiquity. To countless generations of Jews ascent to Jerusalem and residence within its precincts was the highest that life could offer. During eighteen centuries this attachment and this aspiration formed the central theme in the literature of the Jewish people. It was the inspiring force of the numerous Messianic movements which sprang up generation after generation in every part of the far-flung Jewish diaspora. Its reality impressed itself

---

2.

even on the non-Jewish world. Every scheme for a Jewish political restoration in Palestine, from the Proclamation of King Cyrus in the third century B.C.E. to that of Napoleon at the threshold of the nineteenth century was expressed in terms of the rebuilding of Jerusalem. All Jewish prayers for a national restoration, all movements of resettlement, all Messianic aspirations, spiritual and secular, had as their prime object the rebuilding of Jerusalem. Jerusalem came to epitomise Palestine as a whole, its rebuilding became synonymous with the redemption of Israel.

Yet the motive of this age-long attachment is not merely, or even predominantly, political. It would never have survived with such an intensity had it had no deeper inspiration. From its early origins Jerusalem was to the Jew the city of the spirit. David carried into it the Ark of the Covenant and conceived the plan of building a national sanctuary within its walls. King Solomon erected the Temple and thereafter it became the religious centre of the Hebrew people, the city "chosen by God to put his name there". It was not merely the repository of the religious shrine of the nation, but the tribune from which spoke its moral teachers and prophetic guides: "The Lord roareth from Zion and uttereth his voice from Jerusalem" (Amos I,2). In the messages of the prophets it became the emblem of the divine call for the establishment of justice between man and man and between nation and nation. During the last phase of the Jewish State the prophets inspired and comforted the people with the vision of a new world order of universal peace and justice which would arise from a reborn Jerusalem:"And it shall come to pass in the end of days, that the mountain of the Lord's house shall be established in the top of the mountains, and shall be exalted above the hills; and all nations shall flow unto it...For out of Zion shall go forth the law, and the word of the Lord from Jerusalem" (Isaiah II, 2,3). At a later stage this conception was clothed in the mystical

---

3.

vision of a New Jerusalem on high which would one day descend on earth. Nothing, perhaps, is more significant of the depth of the Jewish attachment to Jerusalem than the fact that even in this supernatural projection the vision of a better world was conceived in the image of the beloved city. Nor was the vision allowed to dwarf the reality. A Talmudical saying has it that God will not make his entry into the Jerusalem above before he has returned to the Jerusalem below.* The dictum well exemplifies the distinctive character of that attachment which is spiritual and realistic at once. To the Jewish people Jerusalem is The City. "Aloof, waterless, on the road to nowhere" - such, in the description of George Adam Smith, is the nature of the plateau on which it stands. It has "none of the natural conditions of a great city. And yet it was here that She arose who, more than Athens and/than Rome, taught the nations civic justice, and gave her name to the ideal city men are ever striving to build on earth, to the City of God that shall one day descend from heaven - the New Jerusalem. For her builder was not Nature nor the wisdom of man, but on that secluded and barren site of the Lord of God, by her prophets, laid her eternal foundations in righteousness and reared her walls in her people's faith in God".**

It is by that faith and that attachment that the Jewish People has survived.

---

* Tractate Taanith, p.5

** G.A.Smith: 'The Historical Geography of Palestine", p.319.

abroad and was designed by the Scottish architect Patrick Geddes. Its opening ceremony was attended by the British High Commissioner Sir Herbert Samuel, Professor Chaim Weizmann and Lord Balfour.

Not far from the university is Hadassah Hospital's Mount Scopus branch, established in 1938, and just across the road lies the British War Cemetery on Mount Scopus, the final resting place of thousands of British Empire soldiers who lost their lives in fighting the Ottoman Turks.

There had already been rioting, and attacks on and massacres of Jews in 1921 and 1929. In the 1930s, Arab anger at Jewish immigration boiled over into full-on civil war, with Jews being targeted by several movements engaged in grass-roots anti-British and anti-Zionist activism. These activities were organized by groups such as the Young Men's Muslim Association and the more radical nationalist Hizb al-Istiqlal (Independence Party), which led calls for a boycott of British goods. The more radical activists headed to the hills to take up the fight against the Zionists and British.

In response, the Jews set up their own paramilitary force, the Hagana, to protect Jewish cities, towns, villages and industry. Some groups, such as the Revisionist Zionist Irgun (followers of Vladimir Zee Jabotinski who took a more nationalist line and advocated direct action against the British and Arabs) and the ultra-nationalist Stern Gang, adopted guerrilla tactics against the British as well as fighting the Arabs.

In Jerusalem, the British codified the pink-hued dolomite "Jerusalem Stone" as the urban development standard, one that remains to this day. For all the political turmoil, it was a period that saw a massive building boom in the city as it struggled to cope with the waves of Jewish immigration. Public squares and parks flourished during the Mandate. The British also planned the city's zonal system, determining commercial districts as separate from residential areas.

Some of the city's famous – and now very affluent – neighbourhoods came into their own during this period, including Rechavia (designed by post-Bauhaus architect Richard Kaufman), the German Colony (which was originally the home of a group of German Knights Templar), Talbiya and Bet Hakerem.

Another famous Jerusalem landmark, the YMCA, was built in the early 1930s and was the tallest building in the city at that time. As well as being a sports club, open to all faiths, it hosts cross-communal and multi-faith performances and meetings. Across the street from the YMCA is the King David Hotel, probably Jerusalem's finest, which was opened in 1933.

ARTHUR BALFOUR

Arthur James Balfour (1848–1930), the First Earl of Balfour, was a Conservative politician and statesman who was British Prime Minister between 1902 and 1905, overseeing the series of agreements known as the Entente Cordiale during this time. After losing the 1905 election, he continued as Leader of the Opposition, but eventually resigned from this post in November 1911. Balfour returned to government during the First World War, serving as foreign secretary between 1916 and 1919. It was whilst in this role that he wrote the Balfour Declaration.

BELOW British Conservative politician Arthur James Balfour visiting Jewish colonies in Palestine. His letter as foreign secretary to Lord Rothschild in 1917 paved the way for a Jewish homeland in Palestine.

115

The Second World War

Before the Second World War started in Europe, the Palestinian Arabs were in full revolt against the British Mandate and the Jewish towns and villages they saw as taking up their land.

In 1938, one of the most eccentric British officers ever to don a uniform was dispatched to Jerusalem with the aim of teaching the Jews how to defend themselves – and British interests – better, and how to take the fight to the Arabs. Captain Orde Wingate, a Bible-bashing officer who sided with the Jews because "everyone else was against them", set up shop in the Fast Hotel, just inside the Old City walls near Jaffa Gate. He was regarded as "the friend" by the Zionists, an enemy by the Arabs and a reckless freak by his fellow British officers, mainly because he liked to sit stark naked munching raw onions as he read passages from the Bible.

BELOW Crowds of Palestinian Arabs involved in a riot are dispersed by British troops as part of the revolt against Jewish immigration in 1936.

ABOVE The Bible-bashing Major General Orde C Wingate helped the Jews to set up their own defence forces in Palestine.

During the Arab revolt, which culminated in several Arab fighters taking over the Old City, and the Second World War, Wingate – who has a sports training centre named after him in Israel – trained close to 25,000 Palestinian Jews in the dark commando arts.

The Jews' help for the British almost came to an end after Neville Chamberlain's September 1938 Munich agreement with Hitler. This had the effect of freeing more British troops to guard the Empire's interests in Palestine and meant that the Jews were no longer needed for that role. The Arabs' seizure of the Old City, in October 1938, ended in a bloodbath for the Palestinian Arab nationalists. Although 500 Jews and 150 British soldiers were killed in the revolt, more than 5,000 Arabs died, 146 were sentenced to death, 50,000 were arrested and 5,000 homes were destroyed.

At this point, with war clouds gathering in Europe, Chamberlain decided to try to keep the Arabs on side by reversing the Balfour Declaration. His reasoning was simple: the Jews couldn't back Hitler, but the Arabs might. "If we must offend one side," he said, "let us offend the Jews rather than the Arabs."

Attempts to broker an agreement between the Jews and the Arabs failed, and the Colonial Secretary Malcolm MacDonald issued a White Paper severely curtailing Jewish immigration quotas, to 15,000 annually for five years, after which the Arab nationalists would have a veto. He also stipulated that there would be Palestinian independence in a decade and no Jewish state. It was, by far, the best offer the Palestinians would get, yet their leader, the Mufti of Jerusalem Haj Amin al-Husseini, who was later to strike an alliance with the Nazis (because he believed the Germans would win and drive out the Jews and the British) rejected it out of hand. In fact, the Mufti became very close to Hitler who admired his radical anti-Semitic views, telling him that he was at the forefront of the struggle against "Jewish power". The Nazi leader promised him not only dominion over Palestine and Jerusalem, but over the entire Muslim world. Instead, Al-Husseini was forced to go on the run for most of the war, as he was pursued by British agents from one country to the next.

The Zionist leadership also rejected the White Paper and David Ben-Gurion, then chairman of the Jewish Agency, declared: "We shall fight side by side with the British in our war against Hitler as if there were no White Paper, and we shall fight the White Paper as if there were no war."

During the war, Jerusalem, according to one Arab diarist Hazem Nusseibeh enjoyed "unprecedented peace

and prosperity". The Palestinian Arab nationalists cheered Germany's initial victories, hoping that with the help of Vichy French troops in Syria and Rommel's advance across North Africa, the hated British would be routed and removed.

The Jews, on the other hand, were helping the British, despite the fact that many in the Zionist leadership, including Captain Wingate's main Jewish colleague Moshe Dayan were locked up by Mandate forces since they were seen as terrorists who were agitating for Jewish immigration to Palestine, sometimes by violent means, and this was provoking the Arabs whom the British did not want to upset. As the Axis forces came closer to Palestine, the British decided to release Wingate's trainees and helped set up the Palmach, the Hagana's strike force, to be led by Dayan – who was to lose his eye fighting the Vichy French in Syria – and Yitzhak Sadeh.

Jerusalem became a place of gilded exile for some of the crowned heads of Europe and elsewhere, with George II of Greece, Peter of Yugoslavia and Ethiopia's Haile Selassie all staying at the opulent King David Hotel. An "eat, drink and be merry" atmosphere prevailed in Jerusalem until after Montgomery smashed Rommel's Desert Foxes at el-Alamein in October 1942, only turning sour one month later as news of the full horror of the Holocaust of Europe's Jews started to filter through.

As the news got worse, the Zionists turned their attention to helping Jews escape Nazi-dominated Europe. Some immigrants entered the country on visas issued under the White Paper quota, but the majority came illegally, arriving by land and by sea from Europe and the Middle East.

One of the main problems for the Jews and British in Jerusalem was the Mufti, Haj Amin al-Husseini, the leader of the city's Muslims. Thinking that Adolf Hitler had the war all but won, al-Husseini, a scion of a very ancient Jerusalem family, decided to make common cause with the Fuhrer against the hated Jews and British.

LEFT Adolf Hitler meets with the Grand Mufti of Jerusalem Haj Amin al-Husseini, at the New Reich's Chancellery in Berlin, 9 December 1941. Al-Husseini, an anti-Semite, thought the Fuhrer had the war as good as won and wanted him to help get rid of the Jews in Palestine.

Al-Husseini's anti-British activities made him a target for the Mandate authorities, so he fled to Iran and then on to Italy where he met Benito Mussolini who promised to support his quest for an Arab Muslim state in Palestine. Mussolini also made it clear that Jews had no future in Europe or Palestine, and if they wanted a state of their own, "they should establish Tel Aviv in America".

From il Duce in Rome, the Mufti went to Berlin and met Hitler, just as news was filtering through that the German advance in the Soviet Union had ground to a halt.

Although he failed to extract from Hitler a promise to support his bid for dominion over Palestine, Syria and Iraq, the Mufti made it clear that he shared the Nazi leader's anti-Semitism, hoping that one day there would be "no trace of Zionists... in Palestine".

OPPOSITE Jewish survivors from the Buchenwald Nazi concentration camp aboard a refugee immigration ship on 15 July 1945 at Haifa port.

BELOW The commander of Israel's armed forces in Jerusalem Moshe Dayan reading a map in December 1948.

MOSHE DAYAN

At the beginning of the war, Moshe Dayan (1915–81) was imprisoned because of his activities in the Jewish Palmach paramilitary. But after he was released from prison, he joined the British army and was sent on raids into Syria which was then under control of Vichy France. It was during a skirmish in southern Lebanon that Dayan lifted his binoculars to observe French positions. A bullet smashed through them, lodging itself in his eye-socket and he lost his eye – and from then he was forced to wear his trademark black eye-patch, an item he hated because "it drew attention to myself". With his young wife Ruth, he was sent to Jerusalem to receive treatment and professed a love of walking around the Old City's alleyways. It was, he recalled in his autobiography, "an enchantment".

Statehood and Capital

A s the Second World War ended in 1945, Palestine was once again thrown into the spotlight, with the British having only three years left before their Mandate expired, and the Jews and Arabs fighting each other and the British authorities for supremacy. At the time, Jerusalem had more than 160,000 residents, 100,000 of them Jewish, 34,000 Muslims and the rest Christians.

The fight between the Jews and the Arabs became dirtier, with an increasing level of attacks on civilians, while Jewish extremists, such as Menachem Begin's Irgun and the ultra-nationalist Stern Gang took the fight to the British outside Palestine; the Stern Gang killed Lord Moyne, the British minister resident in Cairo, for suggesting that perhaps a Jewish state should be set up in East Prussia, rather than Palestine.

The British had two proposals for Jerusalem. The first was that it remained British-run in its entirety; the second that it be partitioned, with the United Kingdom controlling the contentious holy sites. Neither the Jews nor the Arabs could agree to either suggestion.

A more pressing problem for the British authorities was the massive influx of Jewish immigrants from the devastation of Europe. Many of the Jews were stuck in displaced persons camps after the Holocaust, too frightened to return to an uncertain future in their previous homelands. The British, still trying to

BELOW Highland Light Infantrymen form a guard of honour observing the departure of the High Commissioner Sir Alan Gordon Cunningham from Jerusalem, 14 May 1948. So ended an era of British rule in Palestine.

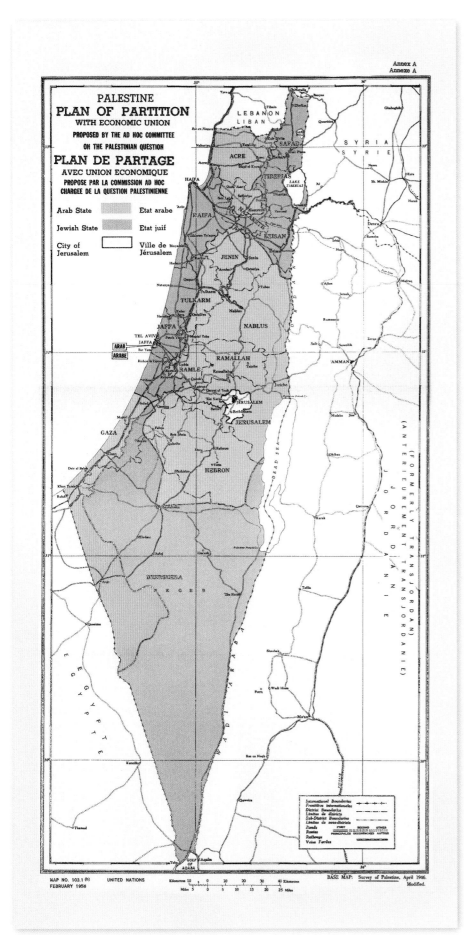

appease the Arabs, refused to allow Jewish immigrants into Palestine, sometimes detaining those who arrived illegally and placing them in detention camps in Cyprus or Eritrea.

Among the ships arriving was the *Exodus* (made famous by the 1960 film starring Paul Newman). The British raided the ship as it approached Palestine's shore and many of those crammed on board, nearly all of whom had barely survived Hitler's camps, were injured. To add insult to injury – or worse – the would-be emigrants were sent back to Germany.

As the conflict in Palestine became more violent, the Jewish paramilitary groups, the Hagana, the Irgun and Stern Gang decided to join forces under a united command to fight the British, and Begin's bombers attacked targets in Jerusalem, including the CID Headquarters and the prison in the Russian Compound, where many of the terrorists were held and interrogated.

Britain needed a way out of the morass and in 1946, an Anglo-American commission of inquiry – based at the King David Hotel where they were surrounded, according to Labour MP Richard Crossman, by "private detectives, Zionist agents, Arab sheikhs, special correspondents all discreetly overhearing each other" – was set up to agree on a policy on the admission of Jews to Palestine. It recommended the immediate acceptance of 100,000 Jewish refugees from Europe into Palestine and that there would be neither an Arab nor a Jewish state. The Committee stated that "in order to dispose, once and for all, of the exclusive claims of Jews and Arabs to Palestine, we regard it as essential that a clear statement of principle should be made that Jew shall not dominate Arab and Arab shall not dominate Jew in Palestine."

The British were finding the Jews hard to handle in Jerusalem. So in June 1946, Viscount Montgomery – the victor of El-Alamein – decided to crack down on the insurgents, launching Operation Agatha (the Jews called it "Black Sabbath") in which 3,000 Jews were arrested. He also turned the Russian Compound into a fortress, which the Jews nicknamed "Bevingrad", after the hated foreign secretary Ernest Bevin, who had demanded a clampdown on Jewish immigration.

LEFT The UN partition plan, voted on and accepted on 29 November 1947. The plan called for the establishment of two states in Palestine – one Jewish, the other Arab, with Jerusalem being internationalized. Although the Zionists accepted the plan, the Arab nationalists didn't and war broke out.

In response, on 26 July 1946, the Irgun and Stern Gang, using 250 kilograms (550 pounds) of explosives hidden in milk churns, blew up a wing of the King David Hotel that housed the British administration and intelligence services. More than 90 people were killed, despite the fact that the terrorists phoned in a warning to the British and to the *Palestine Post* newspaper.

David Ben-Gurion denounced the attack and withdrew the mainstream Jewish Agency and the Hagana from the united command. Britain stepped up its campaign against Jewish insurgents, and banned its soldiers from going to Jewish-owned restaurants and other entertainment places – "to punish the Jews in a way the race dislikes as much as any, by striking their pockets,"according to Sir Evelyn Hugh Barker, the commander of British forces in Palestine. As a further precaution, Britain withdrew all non-military staff from Jerusalem. This marked the start of the Mandate era drawing to a close.

By this point, the Arabs of Jerusalem were becoming increasingly violent in anticipation of the end of British rule. After the United Nations agreed the Palestine Partition Plan in November 1947 – under which Jerusalem would be "internationalized" – militants launched brutal attacks on Jewish targets. Arab mobs lynched Jews and there were demonstrations where the chant "*Itbach al-Yahud*" ("Slaughter the Jews") was constantly heard. Jews were shot in various parts of the city and the Irgun retaliated by lobbing grenades at the Arab bus station near Damascus Gate. Within two weeks of the UN vote, more than 150 people had been killed – 74 Jews, 71 Arabs and 10 British soldiers. The British appeared not to help matters and often sided with the Arabs, or stood aside when the attacks persisted.

Another problem that existed for Jewish Jerusalem – where in the Old City the Jewish Quarter was under siege – was that the main road to the city, past the Kastel Fortress, was under Arab control and supply lorries were often targeted. Although Hagana forces managed to capture the fortress in April 1948, the Arabs retook it days later and in effect blockaded the city.

RIGHT Israel's first prime minister David Ben-Gurion reading Israel's Declaration of Independence to the Meeting of the Constituent Assembly in the Tel Aviv Museum, 14 May 1948. He couldn't get to Jerusalem because of fierce fighting and a siege.

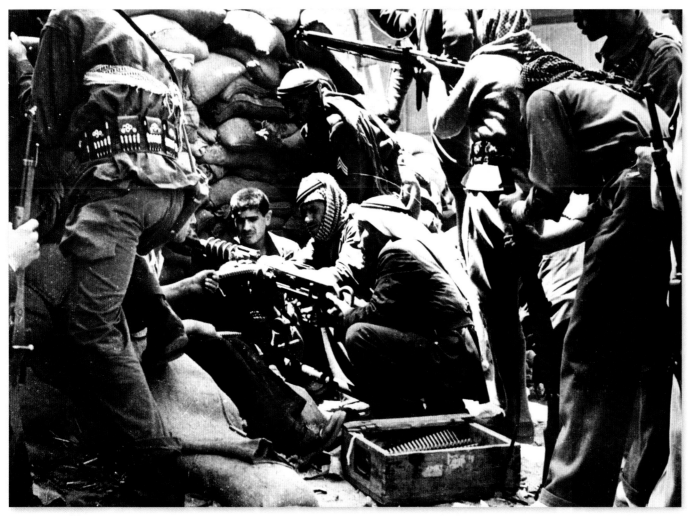

LEFT Soldiers of Allied Arab forces behind a barricade fire on Jewish fighters of the Haganah, the Jewish self-defence force, as they lay siege to Jerusalem, 4 June 1948. The State of Israel was founded on 14 May 1948. The same day, the Arab states of Lebanon, Syria, Jordan, Egypt and Iraq invaded Israel with their regular armies.

OPPOSITE Rachel Levy, a seven-year-old Jewish girl, flees terrified from a street with burning buildings as the Arabs sack the Holy City after its surrender during Israel's War of Independence.

One of the hardest incidents in the war was the battle for the Arab village of Deir Yassin, on the outskirts of Jerusalem, where Irgun irregulars murdered between 100 and 250 civilians (the precise figure has been debated since then) on 9–10 April. David Ben-Gurion apologized to Jordan's King Abdullah (who rejected the apology), and an incensed Arab crowd attacked a convoy of ambulances and food trucks on their way to Hadassah Hospital on Mount Scopus. The attackers photographed themselves with the mutilated bodies of the nurses and doctors who were in the convoy.

The tit-for-tat attacks continued until the British departed Palestine on 15 May 1948, when the State of Israel was declared – an event which took place not in Jerusalem, the capital of the nascent state, but in Tel Aviv, chosen because the situation in Jerusalem was precarious. Supplies were not getting through because of Arab artillery stationed on the main road to the city at Bab el-Wad, the Gate of the Ravine – a bottleneck – and at the Kastel Fortress. There were also more than 5,000 Arab legionaries, well trained by 38 British officers who had just resigned their commission. They were led by General Sir John

Bagot Glubb, who came to be known as Glubb Pasha and commanded the Jordanian Army for many years.

The Arab Legionaries invaded the Corpus Seperatum – the area that was supposed to be under international control according to the 1947 UN partition plan – and invaded Jerusalem, cutting off the Jewish Quarter in the Old City. During the ensuing battles, Jerusalem was divided and the Jews were driven from their Quarter in the Old City and the Jewish State, reborn after 2,000 years, was to be without its holiest site the Western Wall until the 1967 Six-Day War.

Under the 1949 truce, Israel received the west of the city with an ex-territorial island on Mount Scopus, home of the Hadassah Hospital and Hebrew University – both now closed. The hospital reopened in Ein Karem, while the university set up campus in Givat Ram. The Jordanians got the Old City and the West Bank, and although the agreement promised Jews access to the Western Wall, this was never honoured. The area around the western part of the Old City walls was declared no-man's-land and on occasion, Jordanian snipers took pot shots at Israelis from behind the walls at the Mandelbaum Gate.

.2

שארית הפליטה שניצלה מהטבח הנאצי האיום באירופה ויהודי ארצות אחרות לא חדלו להעפיל לארץ ישראל, על אף כל קושי, מניעה וסכנה, ולא פסקו לתבוע את זכותם לחיי כבוד, חירות ועמל-ישרים במולדת עמם.

במלחמת העולם השניה, תרם הישוב העברי בארץ את מלוא-חלקו למאבק האומות, השוחרות חירות ושלום נגד כוחות הרשע הנאצי, ובדם חייליו ובמאמצו המלחמתי קנה לו את הזכות להמנות עם העמים מייסדי ברית האומות המאוחדות.

ב-29 בנובמבר 1947 קיבלה עצרת האומות המאוחדות החלטה המחייבת הקמת מדינה יהודית בארץ-ישראל; העצרת תבעה מאת תושבי ארץ ישראל לאחוז בעצמם בכל הצעדים הנדרשים מצדם הם לביצוע ההחלטה. הכרה זו של האומות המאוחדות בזכות העם היהודי להקים את מדינתו אינה ניתנת להפקעה.

זוהי זכותו הטבעית של העם היהודי להיות ככל עם ועם עומד ברשות עצמו במדינתו הריבונית.

לפיכך נתכנסנו, אנו חברי מועצת העם, נציגי הישוב העברי והתנועה הציונית, ביום סיום המנדט הבריטי על ארץ-ישראל, ובתוקף זכותנו הטבעית וההיסטורית ועל יסוד החלטת עצרת האומות המאוחדות אנו מכריזים בזאת על הקמת מדינה יהודית בארץ-ישראל, היא מדינת ישראל.

אנו קובעים שהחל מרגע סיום המנדט הלילה, אור ליום שבת ו' אייר תש"ח, 15 במאי 1948, ועד להקמת השלטונות הנבחרים והסדירים של המדינה בהתאם לחוקה שתיקבע על-ידי האספה המכוננת הנבחרת לא יאוחר מ-1 באוקטובר 1948 - תפעל מועצת העם כמועצת מדינה זמנית, ומוסד הביצוע שלה, מנהלת-העם, יהווה את הממשלה הזמנית של המדינה היהודית, אשר תיקרא בשם י ש ר א ל.

בארץ ישראל קם העם היהודי, בה עוצבה דמותו הרוחנית, הדתית והמדינית, בה חי חיי קוממיות ממלכתית, בה יצר נכסי תרבות לאומיים וכלל-אנושיים והוריש לעולם כולו את ספר הספרים הנצחי.

לאחר שהוגלה העם מארצו בכוח הזרוע שמר לה אמונים בכל ארצות פזוריו, ולא חדל מתפלה ומתקוה לשוב לארצו ולחדש בתוכה את חירותו המדינית.

מתוך קשר היסטורי ומסורתי זה חתרו היהודים בכל דור לשוב ולהאחז במולדתם העתיקה; ובדורות האחרונים שבו לארצם בהמונים, וחלוצים, מעפילים ומגינים הפריחו נשמות, החיו שפתם העברית, בנו כפרים וערים, והקימו ישוב גדל והולך השליט על משקו ותרבותו, שוחר שלום ומגן על עצמו, מביא ברכת הקידמה לכל תושבי הארץ ונושא נפשו לעצמאות ממלכתית.

בשנת תרנ"ז (1897) נתכנס הקונגרס הציוני לקול קריאתו של הוגה חזון המדינה היהודית תיאודור הרצל והכריז על זכות העם היהודי לתקומה לאומית בארצו.

זכות זו הוכרה בהצהרת בלפור מיום ב' בנובמבר 1917 ואושרה במנדט מטעם חבר הלאומים, אשר נתן במיוחד תוקף בין לאומי לקשר ההיסטורי שבין העם היהודי לבין ארץ-ישראל ולזכות העם היהודי להקים מחדש את ביתו הלאומי.

השואה שנתחוללה על עם ישראל בזמן האחרון, בה הוכרעו מיליונים יהודים באירופה, הוכיחה מחדש בעליל את ההכרח בפתרון בעית העם היהודי מחוסר המולדת והעצמאות על ידי חידוש המדינה היהודית בארץ-ישראל, אשר תפתח לרווחה את שערי המולדת לכל יהודי ותעניק לעם היהודי מעמד של אומה שוות-זכויות בתוך משפחת העמים.

- 3 -

מדינת ישראל תהא פתוחה לעליה יהודית ולקיבוץ גלויות; תשקוד על פיתוח הארץ לטובת כל תושביה; תהא מושתתה על יסודות החירות, הצדק והשלום לאור חזונם של נביאי ישראל; תקיים שויון זכויות חברתי ומדיני גמור לכל אזרחיה בלי הבדל דת וגזע ומין; תבטיח חופש דת, מצפון, לשון, חינוך ותרבות; תשמור על המקומות הקדושים של כל הדתות; ותהיה נאמנה לעקרונותיה של מגילת האומות המאוחדות.

מדינת ישראל תהא מוכנה לשתף פעולה עם המוסדות והנציגים של האומות המאוחדות בהגשמת החלטת העצרת מיום 29 בנובמבר 1947 ותפעל להקמת האחדות הכלכלית של ארץ ישראל בשלמותה.

אנו קוראים לאומות המאוחדות לתת יד לעם היהודי בבנין מדינתו ולקבל את מדינת ישראל לתוך משפחת העמים.

אנו קוראים - גם בתוך התקפת-הדמים הנערכת עלינו זה חדשים - לבני העם הערבי תושבי מדינת ישראל לשמור על השלום וליטול חלקם בבנין המדינה על יסוד אזרחות מלאה ושוה ועל יסוד נציגות מתאימה בכל מוסדותיה, הזמניים והקבועים.

אנו מושיטים יד שלום ושכנות טובה לכל המדינות השכנות ועמיהן, וקוראים להם לשיתוף פעולה ועזרה הדדית עם העם העברי העצמאי בארצו. מדינת ישראל מוכנה לתרום חלקה במאמץ משותף לקידמת המזרח התיכון כולו.

אנו קוראים אל העם היהודי בכל התפוצות להתלכד סביב הישוב בעליה ובבנין ולעמוד לימינו במערכה הגדולה על הגשמת משאת הדורות לגאולת ישראל.

מתוך בטחון בצור ישראל הננו חותמים בחתימת ידינו לעדות על הכרזה זו, במושב מועצת המדינה הזמנית, על אדמת המולדת, בעיר תל-אביב, היום הזה, ערב שבת, ה' אייר תש"ח, 14 במאי 1948.

LEFT AND ABOVE The speech given by David Ben-Gurion when he declared the independence of the State of Israel. (See Translations, page 160.)

However, Jerusalem functioned as Israel's capital, with the Knesset – Israel's Parliament – and most government offices situated there. The Jewish side of the city also developed itself into a cultural centre, with theatres, museums and restaurants.

On the Jordanian side, life also went on, but there was growing hatred towards the Jews and the Jordanians. In July 1951, King Abdullah visited the Old City (after proclaiming that "no one will take over Jerusalem from me unless I am killed") and on the steps of the Dome of the Rock, with his grandson Hussein (later King Hussein of Jordan) by his side, he was shot dead by a Palestinian nationalist. The assassin, angry at the perceived treatment of Palestinians as second-class citizens by the Hashemite Bedouin majority, was himself killed by the king's bodyguards.

The two sides would live in uneasy peace for 19 years in this now hybrid city.

KING ABDULLAH

KING ABDULLAH

King Abdullah of Jordan (1882–1951) supported the right of Jews to set up a national homeland of their own in Palestine – but he wanted to be its ultimate ruler. He supported the 1937 Peel Commission, which proposed dividing Palestine between a Jewish state on 20 per cent of the land and an Arab one on the remainder. He also met Zionist leaders – even when the war was raging – including the future prime minister Golda Meir, whom he beseeched: "Why are you in such a hurry to declare your state? Why don't you wait a few years?" He proposed a Jewish canton in the Hashemite kingdom, but Meir rejected the suggestion.

LEFT Israel's Declaration of Independence, read out by Zionist leader and future first Prime Minister of Israel David Ben-Gurion at the Tel Aviv Museum on 14 May 1948. The declaration says there will be equal rights for all Israeli citizens, irrespective of race, creed, colour or gender. (See Translations, page 160.)

ABOVE King Abdullah and his party standing in front of the Dome of the Rock, a sacred place to Muslims. The king, who favoured talks with Jews, was assassinated there by a Palestinian radical. He was succeeded by his grandson Hussein.

The Tower of David

The building known as the Tower of David, just inside Jaffa Gate at the western entrance to the Old City, probably has nothing to do with King David. It derives its name from the belief of the Byzantines that it really was the palace of the warrior king.

The Tower of David measures approximately 22 metres (72 feet) by 18 metres (59 feet), and consists of 16 courses of large ashlar stones weighing more than a tonne each. Over the past two millennia, it has been destroyed and rebuilt several times by the Romans, the Byzantine and Crusader Christians, Muslims, Mamluks and Ottomans.

The tower and citadel that are now standing date from the second century BC, and were constructed to defend a vulnerable point at the western entrance to the city called the Western Hill, a 770-metre (2,525-feet) -high mound just north of Mount Zion. However, remains of previous fortresses on the point have been found dating back at least 2,700 years (it is thought that King Hezekiah fortified the area in the eighth century BC).

The defences around the Tower were further reinforced under the Hasmonean kings in the second and first centuries BC, who (according to the Jewish-Roman historian Josephus Flavius) built additional walls and watchtowers. Herod, who took control after the Hasmoneans fell, added further walls and towers to protect his palace on Mount Zion.

Extensive archaeological excavations in and around the Tower have revealed the remains of fortifications from the beginning of the first millennium AD. According to Josephus Flavius, the fortifications extended from the citadel itself to the Temple Mount to the east and to the south towards and surrounding Mount Zion.

The wall was first built in this area by Hezekiah, King of Judah, at the end of the eighth century BC. A detailed description of its construction on the eve of the Assyrian invasion of Judah, is in the Bible: "He [Hezekiah] set to work resolutely and built up all the wall that was broken down and raised towers upon it, and outside it he built another wall" (2 Chron. 32:5). The remains of that incredibly wide wall (ca. 7 metres [275 inches]), built of large boulders, were uncovered at great depth on the bedrock of the hill. This mighty fortification protected a new residential quarter built on the southwestern hill of Jerusalem which, until that time, comprised only the City of David and the Temple on Mount Moriah. The wall was damaged in 587/6 BC, when Jerusalem was conquered by the Babylonians.

Remains have also been found in the citadel's courtyard of a Roman legionary camp, including sections from clay water pipes which bear the legionary stamp of the Tenth Legion, the garrison which controlled the city: "L X F", which stands for "Legio X Fretensis".

The tallest of the towers, the 35-metre (115-feet) high Phasael – which still stands today – was named after Herod's brother. Two other towers, one called Miriamne after his second wife, whom he had executed, and another named Hippicus, after one of his friends, no longer exist.

When the Romans conquered the city in AD 70, the tower was turned into a barracks. And after the Romans adopted Christianity in the fourth century, the citadel became a monastery. The Arabs refurbished and fortified the citadel after their conquest in AD 638 to such an extent that it became a serious obstacle for the Crusaders in 1099 and only fell after assurances they could leave the city unharmed. The Crusaders added a moat and more battlements to protect pilgrims who were reaching the city from the west – from the post of Jaffa, about 60 kilometres (37 miles) away.

The Mamluks destroyed the building in 1260, but later rebuilt it. The Ottomans refurbished and strengthened it between 1537 and 1541, establishing a cannon emplacement and using the citadel as a base for their garrison in the city, and adding a mosque and a minaret.

When General Edmund Allenby captured Jerusalem on behalf of the British Army in late 1917, he used the Tower of David as the place from which to proclaim his victory. And during the period of British rule (both pre-Mandate and Mandate) from 1918 to 1948, the British High Commission's Pro-Jerusalem Society (a body established to ensure the city's cultural heritage was safeguarded) cleaned and renovated the building, and used it as a concert and exhibition venue. It also served as a museum for Palestinian folklore.

When the Arab Legion captured the building in 1948, during the first Arab-Israeli War, they reverted it back to its old role as a citadel because of its commanding views of the Western part of the city which was in Israeli hands. In June

OPPOSITE The Tower of David has been renovated on many occasions. It is now home to a museum of archaeological artefacts.

OVERLEAF The Jaffa Gate, just next to the Tower of David, is usually the first sight tourists see of the Old City.

COOKS
TOURIST OFFICE
INSIDE JAFFA GATE

1967, when the Israelis captured the Old City in the Six-Day War, it became a cultural centre and museum again. It is usually the first building tourists see as they enter the Old City from the Jaffa Gate.

The building now houses The Tower of David Museum of the History of Jerusalem, which was opened in 1989 by the Jerusalem Foundation (a fundraising organization set up to preserve the city's cultural heritage) and displays archaeological artefacts going back over the city's 5,000 years.

Jerusalem's New Institutions

When Teddy Kollek was elected mayor of West Jerusalem in 1965, the city's Jewish half – of which he was mayor – was a provincial backwater with little in the way of cultural life. When he finally lost his position after five re-elections (to his right-wing Likud rival Ehud Olmert) in 1993, the city had become the largest in Israel in terms of size and population, and had a cultural life to rival Tel Aviv's.

Described by many as the greatest builder of Jerusalem since King Herod, Hungarian-born Kollek in an interview with the *New York Times* once said: "I got into this by accident[...] I was bored. When the city was united [after the 1967 Six-Day War, when Israel annexed the Arab East and the Old City], I saw this as an historic occasion. To take care of it and show better care than anyone else ever has is a full life purpose. I think Jerusalem is the one essential element in Jewish history. A body can live without an arm or a leg, not without the heart. This is the heart and soul of it."

Kollek was responsible for many cultural projects and institutions during the almost 30 years that he served in office. He was the brains and the moving force behind the development and expansion of the Israel Museum. As the museum's founder, he served as its president for almost the entire period of his mayoralty, from 1965–96. When this museum – which houses, among many other things, the Dead Sea Scrolls – celebrated its twenty-fifth anniversary in 1990, Kollek was given the honorific title "Avi Ha-muze'on" ("the father of the museum").

The museum is the largest cultural institution in Israel and is considered to be one of the world's most important art and archaeology museums. Founded in 1965, it houses comprehensive collections, estimated at about 500,000 objects, including works dating from prehistory to the present day, and features the most extensive holdings of biblical and Holy Land archaeology in the world.

Among the highlights of the museum's original campus is the Shrine of the Book, designed by Armand Bartos and Frederick Kiesler, which houses the Dead Sea Scrolls – the oldest Biblical manuscripts in the world – as well as a collection of rare early medieval Biblical texts.

RIGHT The mayor of Jerusalem Teddy Kollek taking a tour of the city. In his five terms, he did much to promote Jerusalem as an international centre of arts and culture.

ABOVE The Community Rule scroll (Qumran, cave 1), c.100 BC–AD 100, housed in the Israel Museum.

OPPOSITE The Dead Sea Scrolls, discovered between 1947 and 1956 by Israeli archaeologist Yigael Yadin, revealed a lot about the way of life in Jerusalem in Roman times. This is part of one of the scrolls found by Yadin in 1960 in what became known as the Cave of Letters, located in the Dead Sea area. This was the largest amount of ancient documents and personal letters ever discovered in Israel and included papers written by Shimon Bar Kokhba, the leader of the Third Jewish Revolt against Rome (132–135 CE). Following the First Jewish-Roman War 66–73 CE, Roman control over the Judea was tightened, leading to tensions with the Jewish people. Shimon Bar Kokhba was believed by many to be a Jewish Messiah who could restore Israel to its former glory. Initially the revolt was successful and established an independent state of Israel over parts of Judea, but eventually the revolt was put down and the Jews were banned from entering Jerusalem. After the Revolt, most Jews in Judea were treated even more harshly than before as they were killed, exiled or made into slaves and Jewish religious and political authority was also severely curtailed.

Beside the Shrine, a model of Jerusalem during the Second Temple period has been set up. It displays the layout and architecture of the city before it was destroyed by the Romans after the AD 66 uprising, providing valuable historical context to the presentation of the Dead Sea Scrolls.

Kollek once remarked that Israel needed a strong army, but it also needed expressions of culture and civilization. As part of this, he was behind the establishment of the Jerusalem Theatre, and in 1966 established the Jerusalem Foundation, an international non-profit organization whose goal is the improvement of the quality of life for all citizens of the city. Through the foundation, millions of pounds have been raised to enhance the cultural life of Jerusalem.

Kollek was also instrumental in developing the city's Biblical Zoo, which originally occupied a 6-hectare (15-acre) site in the centre of the city. Although it attracted many visitors to its exhibits of animals, reptiles and birds mentioned in the Bible, and was successful in breeding and protecting endangered species, the site was too small. Under, Kollek it moved to a larger location near the Teddy Stadium (the footbal stadium, also named after Kollek) and became a state-of-the-art institution where animals could roam in larger areas. It is now on a 25-hectare (62-acre) expanse near the neighbourhood Malha. Kollek helped raise the funds to allow the zoo to build a new enclosure for its elephants, and Kollek helped the zoo raise money to build a new elephant enclosure and to bring in elephants from Thailand (an operation which cost $50,000 per animal). A male was named Teddy and a female elephant Tamar in honour of the mayor and his wife.

But the greatest event in Kollek's mayoralty was the 1967 Six-Day War, when Israel captured the east of the city from Jordan and with it acquired hundreds of thousands of Arab inhabitants. Kollek was nothing if not pragmatic, although some Israelis thought him pro-Arab. Within hours of Israel's capture of the Arab neighourhoods, he ordered that Arab children would be provided with milk. But, on the other hand, he was instrumental in the destruction of Jerusalem's Moroccan quarter, a clearance operation which rendered 100 families homeless. The Moroccan Quarter stood in front of the Western Wall and included several schools and religious institutions. Its demolition by the Israeli government was ordered to make public access to the Western Wall easier.

RIGHT The Shrine of the Book, the wing of the Israel Museum where the Dead Sea Scrolls are kept.

Kollek's advocacy of tolerance in religious matters was demonstrated by his frequent attempts while mayor to engage with the Arab community. Muslim access to the al-Aqsa Mosque and the al-Haram ash-Sharif (The Temple Mount) was protected, and he also opposed the establishment of new Jewish neighbourhoods in the heart of the Arab part of the city. After he left office, Kollek became increasingly concerned about the treatment of the city's Arabs and believed that they should be given self-rule.

Towards the end of his reign as a mayor of Jerusalem, he stated that Israel's Arab population had remained "second- and third-class citizens" and that neither he nor other Israeli leaders had done anything to improve the Arabs' rights or quality of life. In an interview with the Israeli *Haaretz* daily, he was typically forthright:

"We said things half-mindedly and never fulfilled them. We've said again and again that we will make Arabs' rights equal those of the Jews – empty words... both [Prime Minister Levi] Eshkol and [Prime Minister Menachem] Begin promised equal rights – both broke their promises... they [Palestinians] were and remain second and third class citizens."

He acknowledged also that he hadn't done enough for the Arabs of his city: "Nonsense! Fables! Never built nor developed! I did do something for Jewish Jerusalem in the last 25 years. But for eastern Jerusalem, what did we do? Nothing! What did I do? Schools? Nothing! Pavements? Nothing! Culture centres? Not one! We did give them sewage and improved the water supply. You know why? You think [we did it] for their own good? For their quality of life? No way! There were a few cases of cholera and the Jews were scared that it might reach them, so we installed sewage and water... We failed in the unification of the city."

LEFT The Jerusalem Centre for the Performing Arts.

ABOVE A baby giraffe named Nill, who was born at the Jerusalem Biblical Zoo in February 2004.

143

The Six-Day War

In May and June 1967, the Middle East was on tenterhooks. The Egyptian president Gamal Abdul-Nasser was raising the political temperature in the region with inflammatory rhetoric and many Israelis feared that their country would be over-run.

On 16 May, Nasser, believing the Israelis were preparing to mount an attack on Syria, ordered the removal of the United Nations Emergency Force, which had kept the peace in the region since the 1956 Suez war, from the Sinai desert and started moving his troops to the border with Israel.

On 22–23 May, he closed the Straits of Tiran at the southern tip of Sinai to Israeli shipping. This was viewed by Israel as *casus belli* and after the Egyptian leader declared on 26 May that his intention was to destroy Israel, the country's leaders prepared for

the worst. On 5 June 1967, Israeli Air Force jets launched pre-emptive strikes in Egypt and Syria, destroying both countries' air forces on the ground. In effect, the war was over.

Israel hoped the Jordanians would not enter the 1967 Six-Day War. Official records show that Israeli officials, who had developed relatively close ties with the Harrow-educated King Hussein of Jordan because of their mutual suspicion of the Palestinians, tried many times to dissuade the young monarch from joining forces with Gamal Abdul-Nasser's Egypt and Syria, but to no avail.

Hussein's calculation was different, and despite not believing the Egyptian president's bravado in asserting that Israel was on the verge of destruction, he felt that if Nasser lost, he would be regarded as a traitor.

LEFT Israeli soldiers on the Via Dolorosa in the Old City. Despite pleas from Israeli leaders not to enter the war, King Hussein of Jordan sided with Egypt's Gamal Abd-al Nasser and lost East Jerusalem and the West Bank.

OPPOSITE General Moshe Dayan (front left), Yitzhak Rabin and other military representatives take a tour through the Old City in Jerusalem after its capture.

At first the Israelis were worried that the Jordanians would take advantage of the fact that Israeli forces were mainly deployed and fighting against the Egyptians in the south. They feared that the Jordanians would encircle the western part of Jerusalem, which was not heavily defended, and lay siege to its 200,000 residents.

Acting on instructions from the Egyptians, and despite pleas from the Israelis that they had no plans to attack, at 11.15 a.m. on 5 June the Jordanian artillery opened up a massive barrage – some estimate that more than 6,000 shells were fired.

Israel responded only with small arms, on the orders of defence minister Moshe Dayan, and offered a ceasefire that the Jordanians rejected thinking that the Israelis were in a weakened position. Dayan was reportedly not keen on conquering the city, as its political and religious complexities could be a millstone around Israel's neck for years to come. However, he was overruled and on 6 June at 2.10 a.m., Israeli paratroopers under the command of General Uzi Narkis and Colonel Mordechai (Motta) Gur marched on the Old City and the eastern sector. They encountered strong Jordanian resistance, especially at Ammunition Hill, the Mandelbaum Gate and the American Colony Hotel. However, all three positions fell by 7.30 a.m.

With the UN debating a ceasefire on 7 June, the Israeli government, and especially the hawks such as Herut leader (and former Irgun chief) Menachem Begin, who had joined before the war, realized time was running out to capture the Old City and the Western Wall.

Israeli paratroopers swiftly captured the Mount of Olives to the east of the Old City, and started moving towards the Garden of Gethsemane just outside the walls. The troops burst through the walls and Colonel Gur made one of the most famous military broadcasts in Israeli history: "The Temple Mount is in our hands." Gur's paratroopers were later joined by other forces that had broken through Jordanian lines elsewhere in the Old City and the battle for Jerusalem was effectively over. At 2.30 p.m., barely 12 hours after the offensive had started, Narkis, Dayan and the Israeli chief of staff Yitzhak Rabin entered the old city.

Dayan, on seeing an Israeli flag atop the Dome of the Rock, ordered its immediate removal, saying he did not want to offend Muslim sensibilities. And that set the tone for most of the period after the war. Despite the Old City having come under Israeli control, the Temple Mount, with its two sacred mosques, were left in the hands of the Muslim Waqf, an Islamic trust.

Israel set about clearing the area in front of the Western Wall, removing the Mughrabi (Moroccan) Quarter, so that Jews could gain access. However, it also let the other religions run their own affairs and did not change some of the centuries-old arrangements for the administering of the religious sites in the city.

PREVIOUS PAGES Israeli soldiers celebrating their capture of Old Jerusalem in front of the Dome of the Rock on 11 June 1967.

BELOW Arab soldiers surrender to Israeli forces in the occupied West Bank on 13 June 1967.

OPPOSITE Israeli troops standing outside buildings in the Old City of Jerusalem that had been damaged during the Six-Day War.

Jerusalem's Cultural Life

If you walk down Rechov Ha'Nevi'im – the Street of the Prophets – in central Jerusalem, you will see just how diverse the city has become since the Israeli capture of the eastern part in 1967.

You are very likely to pass pious ultra-Orthodox Jews as they make their way from the neighbouring Meah She'arim quarter, where visiting non-religious people are advised to dress modestly to avoid causing offence.

You will also encouter priests from the nearby Ethiopian and Coptic churches as they make their way in ceremonial clothing to or from the Old City and its monasteries and houses of worship.

And, almost side-by-side, Palestinian Arabs from the East of the city will encouter young, secular and hip Israelis making their way to some of the non-kosher eateries in the area. There will also be a smattering of burly soldiers too. Rehov haNevi'im, you see, is a micro-cosm of Jerusalem.

Immediately after the 1967 Six-Day War, Jews around the world rejoiced, not least because fears that Israel was about to be annihilated only 19 years after its creation and 22 years after the Holocaust were unfounded. Orthodox and most secular Jews had further reason to rejoice – the city of Jerusalem, divided since the 1949 Armistice Agreement with Jordan, was under complete Israeli control for the first time. Jews could once again visit their holy sites in the Old City, eastern suburbs and villages.

BELOW After the Six-Day War, Jerusalem's Western Wall was restored to Jewish control and became once more a place for Jews to gather in prayer, as this image by Leonard Freed shows.

RIGHT This Claus Oldenburg sculpture is located outside the entrance to the main gallery of the Israel Museum. After a $10-million renovation, the museum reopened to the public in July 2010.

ABOVE The Israel Philharmonic Orchestra performs at the opening of the Jerusalem Museum at the Jaffa Gate.

OPPOSITE A poster advertising a French exhibition about Jerusalem, entitled "Metaphors and Allegories of Jerusalem" and was shown at the French Pompidou Centre in Paris 1978. In recent years exhibitions on the culture and heritage of Jerusalem have become common all over the world, showing the world's interest in the Holy City.

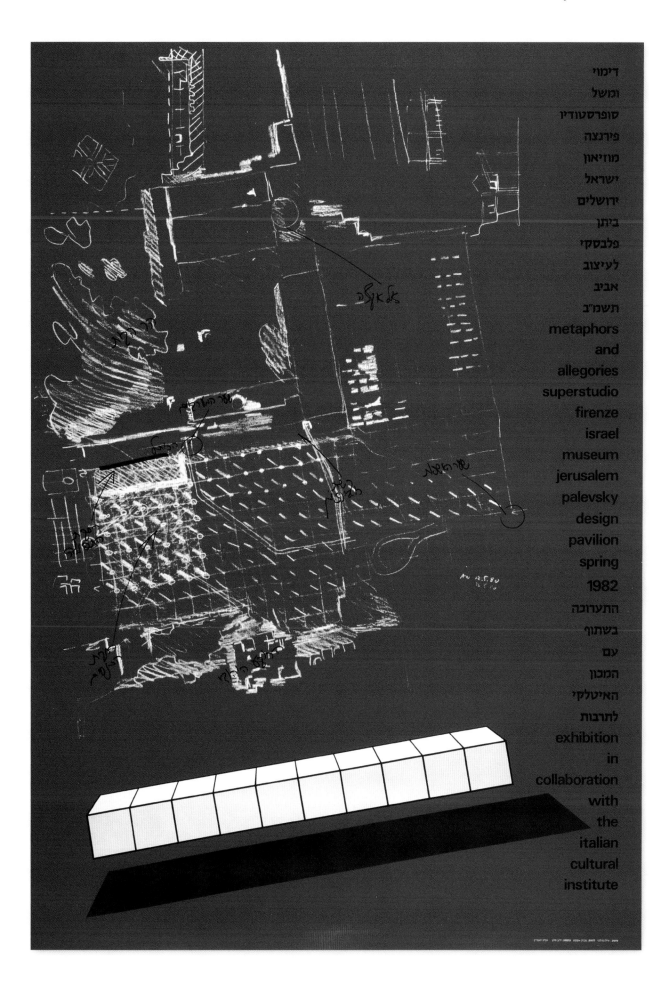

Unfortunately, however, Jerusalem's capture and reunification spawned two diametrically and violently opposed reactions. Some Jews saw the recapture as the beginning of a Messianic era, and started building suburbs in the heart of Arab neighbourhoods. Often protected by Israeli soldiers, these settlers believed – and in fact still do believe – that by building and expanding in Jerusalem they are hastening the coming of the anointed one. As successive Israeli governments have seen building and expanding in Jerusalem as a national priority, the settlers have no reason to believe otherwise.

Opposite them are alienated and angry Muslims, who feel that they are being shunted out of their city, which they regard as the third holiest in Sunni Islam. First carried by Gamal Abdul Nasser's pan-Arabism and Palestinian nationalism, they are now becoming increasingly supportive of fundamentalist movements such as Hamas, the Palestinian wing of the Egyptian Muslim Brotherhood.

The situation has become so tense that Israel, after declaring that it would not allow separation and dividing walls to be built in the city after 1967, has built one such wall that it calls a security barrier, which scars Jerusalem's skyline.

However, there is still much for Jerusalem's over one million residents to celebrate. It used to be said that Jerusalem's cultural life began at the city's exit – on the main road to Tel Aviv, where all the top restaurants, theatres, museums and, of course, a beach, attracted the city's mainly secular and modern Orthodox elite.

Not any more. Today, people are more likely to travel from the coastal plain to Jerusalem to sample its cultural fare. Jerusalem is home to thousands of restaurants, catering for all tastes, from traditional East European Jewish to the latest fusion trends, via some of the best Middle Eastern cuisine.

The city has its own cinematheque – nestling in a beautiful park under the Old City walls near Mount Zion – which for the past 30 years has been running an annual film festival in the summer that has attracted top Hollywood stars. The festival runs feature films and documentaries and hands out its own "Oscars".

For opera lovers, there is also an annual festival which brings top singers and orchestras to Israel to sing arias against the historical backdrops of the Old City walls or the historical churches. The Tower of David Citadel has also been used as a fantastic setting.

Apart from the Israel Museum with its exhibition of the Dead Sea Scrolls in the Shrine of the Book and its displays of ancient and contemporary art, Jerusalem is also home to a number of other museums, such as the Bible Lands Museum, which houses a unique collection of artefacts depicting the cultures and civilizations of the Near East. For the archaeology buff, there is the Rockefeller Museum just outside Damascus Gate. It has a huge collection of artefacts found during excavations at the time of the British Mandate.

Jerusalem is home to a botanical garden that has more than 6,000 plant species from all over the world. It doubles up as a research centre that looks into how plants adapt to Jerusalem's climate (which is mainly dry and hot). The city also has a Biblical zoo, originally established in 1940 as a little children's zoo but now stretches across a 25-hectare (62-acre) park in a beautiful valley. The zoo is home to all the animals mentioned in the Bible – biblical references are

displayed by each enclosure – and even some that are not, such as penguins.

The sprawling city, the largest in area terms in Israel, (Greater Jerusalem takes up 647 square kilometres [250 square miles], including new Israeli suburbs and neighbourhoods built on land occupied since the 1967 Six-Day War) has a comprehensive public transport system to which a new urban light railway has been added.

But this too has not been without its political problems, with Palestinians complaining that it cuts through their neighbourhoods which they hope one day will be part of their own state's capital.

In Jerusalem, everything is politics.

OVERLEAF The view on the cupola of the Hall of Names at Yad Vashem, Israel's national Holocaust Memorial, in Jerusalem. School children are often taken to the memorial to remind them why a Jewish state is necessary.

BELOW During a eight-day tour of the Holy Land in May 2009, Pope Benedict XVI pays a visit to Yad Vashem to lay a wreath in memory of the six million Jews who lost their lives in the Holocaust. This image shows the Pontiff praying over the Eternal Flame.

YAD VASHEM

One of Jerusalem's most famous museums is Yad Vashem, Israel's memorial to the six million Jews who perished in the Holocaust. The museum's hall of remembrance is graced by heads of state and government when they visit Israel. It is home to the largest and most comprehensive repository of material on the Holocaust in the world, with 58 million pages of documents and nearly 100,000 still photographs, along with thousands of films and videotaped testimonies of survivors.

INDEX

Page numbers in *italic* type refer to illustrations or their captions.

MEMORABILIA CREDITS

The publishers would like to thank the following sources for their kind permission to reproduce the pictures in this book.

Key, T=top, L=left, R=right, B=bottom

Bridgeman Images: Church of Saint Gaorge, Ma'daba, Jordan/Photo © Zev Radovan: 23; /Ken Welsh: 48; / Centre Historique des Archives Nationales/ Giraudon: 105

The Central Zionist Archives: 91; 111

Centre Pompidou: /MNAM-CCI, Dist. RMN/Georges Meguerditchian: 153

Corbis: /Sotheby's/Reuters: 109; /Donald Nausbaum/Robert Harding World Imagery: 139r

The Israel State Archives: 114; 128; 129l

Public domain: 79t

Royal Geographical Society (with IBG): 67

Topfoto.co.uk: 104

The United Nations: 123

PICTURE CREDITS

The publishers would like to thank the following sources for their kind permission to reproduce the pictures in this book.

Key, t=top, l=left, r=right, b=bottom

Akg-Images: 32–33, 35; /Cameraphoto: 62; /Gerard Degeorge: 102; / Israelimages: 83, 84-85; /Erich Lessing: 50, 61; /Ullstein Bild: 118–119

Alamy Images: Nir Alon: 142-143; /The Art Archive: 77; /Russell Kord: 140-141; /Peter M. Wilson: 53

Art Archive: Pharaonic Village Cairo/Gianni Dagli Orti: 59

Bridgeman Images: Archives Charmet/Bibliotheque Nationale: 76-77; / Bibliotheque Nationale: 63; /Centre Historique des Archives Nationales/ Giraudon: 105; / The Israel Museum: 138-139; /Look and Learn: 14; / Corporal Henry Phillips/Palestine Exploration Fund: 19; /Private Collection: 3; /Zev Radovan: 18-19, 23

The Central Zionist Archives: 91, 111

© Centre Pompidou, MNAM-CCI, Dist, RMN/Georges Meguerditchian: 153

Corbis: 113, 117; /Alinari Archives: 9; /Noam Armonn/Spaces Images: 131; / Bettmann: 29r, 68-69, 74, 94-95, 122, 146-147; /Heritage Images: 56, 70; /Chris Hellier: 71; /Historical Picture Archive: 12; /Jim Hollander/epa: 81; / Hulton-Deutsch Collection: 87r, 95, 134; /Judy Lash Balint/Demotix: 151; / Peter Kneffel/dpa: 156-157; /David Lees: 57; /Donald Nausbaum/Robert Harding: 139; /World Imagery; /Richard T. Nowitz: 152; / Fred de Noyelle/ Godong: 22; /Leonard de Selva: 58; /Sotheby's/Reuters: 109; /Antoine Gyori/Sygma: 54-55

Getty Images: 8, 28, 29l, 36, 37, 40, 42-43, 60, 79b, 88, 98, 101, 106-107, 108, 112, 116, 120, 149, 154-155; /AFP: 127, 143, 148; /Alinari: 11; / Bridgeman Images: 44; /National Geographic: 38-39; /SuperStock: 47, 51; /Time & Life Pictures: 16-17, 92-93, 121, 126, 129r, 136-137

The Israel State Archives: 114, 128, 129l

Magnum Photos Ltd: /Leonard Freed: 150

Mary Evans Picture Library: /Grovsenor Prints: 73; /Rue des Archives/ Tallandier: 97

Musée du Louvre: 13

Photo12: 110; /Ann Ronan Picture Library: 89. 99, 115; /Hachedé: 96

© Royal Geographical Society (with IBG): 67

Thinkstock.com: 80-81

Topfoto.co.uk: 14, 24, 26-27, 30, 31, 66, 75, 104, 124-125; /Dan Porges/ ArenaPAL: 87t, 87b; /Duby Tal/Albatross: 5, 82; /Artmedia/HIP: 34-35; / Fine Art Images/Heritage-Images: 49; /The Granger Collection: 21, 52; / Dallas & John Heaton: 103; /Jorge Novominsky: 64-65; /Luisa Ricciarini: 68; /Ullsteinbild: 10-11, 132-133, 144, 145; /World History Archive: 45, 72, 78

The United Nations: 123

Every effort has been made to acknowledge correctly and contact the source and/or copyright holder of each picture and Carlton Books Limited apologises for any unintentional errors or omissions which will be corrected in future editions of this book.

TRANSLATIONS

Page 128 Ben-Gurion's speech

The Jewish people came into being in Eretz Israel (the Land of Israel). Here their spiritual, religious and political identity was shaped. Here they first achieved statehood, created cultural values of national and universal significance, and gave to the world the eternal Book of Books.

After being forcibly exiled from their land, the people remained faithful to it throughout their Dispersion and never ceased to pray and hope for their return to it and for the restoration in it of their political freedom.

Impelled by this historic and traditional attachment, Jews strove in every successive generation to re-establish themselves in their ancient homeland. In recent decades they returned in their masses. Pioneers, immigrants coming to the Land of Israel despite restrictive legislation, and defenders, they made deserts bloom, revived the Hebrew language, built villages and towns, and created a thriving community controlling its own economy and culture, loving peace but knowing how to defend itself, bringing the blessings of progress to all the country's inhabitants, and aspiring towards independent nationhood.

In the year 5657 (1897), answering the call of the spiritual father of the Jewish State, Theodor Herzl, the First Zionist Congress convened and proclaimed the right of the Jewish people to national rebirth in its own country.

This right was recognized in the Balfour Declaration of 2 November 1917, and reaffirmed in the Mandate of the League of Nations which, in particular, gave international sanction to the historic connection between the Jewish people and Eretz Israel and to the right of the Jewish people to rebuild its National Home.

The catastrophe which recently befell the Jewish people -- the massacre of millions of Jews in Europe -- was another clear demonstration of the urgency of solving the problem of its homelessness by re-establishing the Jewish State in Eretz-Israel. This would open the gates of the homeland wide to every Jew and confer upon the Jewish people the status of a fully privileged member of the comity of nations.

Survivors of the Nazi holocaust in Europe, as well as Jews from other parts of the world, continued to migrate to Eretz-Israel, undaunted by difficulties, restrictions and dangers, and never ceased to assert their right to a life of dignity, freedom and honest toil in their national homeland.

In the Second World War, the Jewish community of this country contributed its full share to the struggle of the freedom- and peace-loving nations against the forces of Nazi evil and, by the blood of its soldiers and its war effort, gained the right to be reckoned among the peoples which founded the United Nations.

On 29 November, 1947, the United Nations General Assembly passed a resolution calling for the establishment of a Jewish State in Eretz Israel; the General Assembly required the inhabitants of Eretz-Israel to take such steps as were necessary for the implementation of that resolution. This recognition by the United Nations of the right of the Jewish people to establish their State is irrevocable.

This right is the natural right of the Jewish people to be masters of their own fate in their own sovereign State, like all other nations.

Accordingly we, members of the People's Council, representatives of the Jewish community of Eretz Israel and of the Zionist movement, are here assembled on the day of the termination of the British Mandate over Eretz Israel and, by virtue of our natural and historic right and on the strength of the resolution of the United Nations General Assembly, hereby declare the establishment of a Jewish State in Eretz Israel, to be known as the State of Israel.

We declare that, with effect from the moment of the termination of the Mandate tonight, the eve of Sabbath, 6 Iyar, 5708 (15 May, 1948), until the establishment of the elected, regular authorities of the State in accordance with the Constitution which shall be adopted by the Elected Constituent Assembly not later than 1 October 1948, the People's Council shall act as a Provisional Council of State, and its executive organ, the People's Administration, shall be the Provisional Government of the Jewish State, to be called "Israel".

The State of Israel will be open to Jewish immigration and the gathering of the Exiles; will foster the development of the country for the benefit of all its inhabitants; will be based on freedom, justice and peace as envisaged by the prophets of Israel; will ensure complete equality of social and political rights to all its inhabitants irrespective of religion, race or sex; will guarantee freedom of religion, conscience, language, education and culture; will safeguard the Holy Places of all religions, and will be faithful to the principles of the Charter of the United Nations.

The State of Israel is prepared to co-operate with the agencies and representatives of the United Nations in implementing the resolution of the General Assembly of 29 November, 1947, and will take steps to bring about the economic union of the whole of Eretz Israel.

We appeal to the United Nations to assist the Jewish people in building up its State and to receive the State of Israel into the comity of nations.

We appeal – in the very midst of the attack being conducted against us for months now -- to the Arab inhabitants of the State of Israel to preserve peace and participate in building up the State on the basis of full and equal citizenship and due representation in all its provisional and permanent institutions.

We extend our hand to all neighbouring states and their peoples in an offer of peace and good neighbourliness, and appeal to them to establish bonds of co-operation and mutual help with the sovereign Jewish people settled in its own land. The State of Israel is prepared to do its share in a common effort for the advancement of the entire Middle East.

We appeal to the Jewish people throughout the Diaspora to rally round the Jews of Eretz Israel in the tasks of immigration and up-building, and to stand by them in the great struggle for the realization of the age-old dream -- the redemption of Israel.

Placing our trust in the Rock of Israel [God], we affix our signatures to this Proclamation at this session of the Provisional Council of State, on the soil of the homeland, in the city of Tel Aviv, on this Sabbath eve, the 5th day of Iyar, 5708 (14 May, 1948).

Page 129 Declaration of Independence

Eretz-Israel [in Hebrew, The Land of Israel] was the place of birth for the Jewish people. It was here that their spiritual, religious and identity was formed. Here they first achieved statehood, established cultural values that were of national and universal importance and gave the world the eternal Book of Books.

After being forced to leave their land. the Jewish people retain their faith in it throughout their Dispersion and never gave up praying and hoping that they would be able to return to it and that their political freedom would be restored there.

Compelled by this historic and traditional association, every generation of Jewish people attempted to return to their homeland. In recent decades, the Jews returned in their masses. Immigrants who came in defiance of prohibitive laws and defenders, they mad the deserts flourish, revived the Hebrew language, created towns and villages and built a thriving community which was in charge of its economy and culture, desiring peace but also knowing how to defend itself, bringing the gifts of progress to all those who inhabited the land, and aiming for independent nationhood.

In 1897, at the behest of Theodor Herzl, the Jewish state's spiritual fat he, the First Zionist Congress was convened and announced the right of the Jews to a national rebirth in its own country.

This right was acknowledged in the Balfour Declaration on 2 November 1917 and was then reasserted in the Mandate of the League of Nations. The latter also gave international agreement on the historic connection between Jews and Eretz-Israel and the right of the Jews to rebuild their National Home.

The disaster that recently blighted the Jewish people – the massacre of millions of Jewish people in Europe – showed again the importance of solving the issue of its homelessness by reestablishing Eretz-Irsael in the Jewish State, which would allow every Jewish person access to the homeland and also bestow up the Jews the standing of being a fully acknowledged member of the comity of nations.

Survivors of the Holocaust in Europe, as well as Jews elsewhere in the world, still migrated to Eretz-Israel, refusing to be deterred by the problems, restrictions and potential risks, and never stopped affirming their right to a life of dignity, freedom and honest work in their national homeland.

During the Second World War, the Jewish people of this country contributed their full quota to the fight of freedom- and peace-loving nations against the forces of Nazi evil and, through the sacrifice of its soldiers and its war effort, achieved the right to be counted among the people who founded the League of Nations.

On 29 November 1947, the United Nations General Assembly passed a resolution that asked for the establishment of a Jewish State in Eretz-Israel; the General Assembly asked the people of Eretz-Irsael to take the steps required of them in order that this resolution be implemented. The recognition of the United nations of the right of the Jews to establish their State cannot be revoked.

This right is the natural right of the Jews to be in control of their own fate, live other nations, in their sovereign State.

ACCORDINGLY WE, MEMBERS OF THE PEOPLE'S COUNCIL, REPRESENTATIVES OF THE JEWISH PEOPLE OF ERETZ-ISRAEL AND OF THE ZIONIST MOVEMENT, ARE ASSEMBLED ON THE DAY OF THE END OF THE BRITISH MANDATE OVER ERETZ-IRSAEL AND, BECAUSE OF OUR NATURAL AND HISTORIC RIGHT AND THE RESOLUTION OF THE UNITED NATIONS GENERAL ASSEMBLY, HEREBY DECLARE THE ESTABLISHMENT OF A JEWISH STATE IN ERETZ-ISRAEL, TO BE CALLED THE STATE OF ISRAEL.

WE DECLARE that, from the moment of the end of the Mandate, tonight, the eve of the Sabbath, in the 6th lyra, 5708 (15 May 1948), until the formation of the elected, regular authorities of the State in line with the Constitution which shall be adopted by the Elected Constituent Assembly not later than 1 October 1948, the People's Council shall act as a Provisional Council of State, and its executive arm, the People's Administration, shall be the Provisional Government of the Jewish State, to be named "Israel".

THE STATE OF ISRAEL will be open for Jewish immigration and the gathering of the Exiles; it will encourage the development of the country for the benefit of all its citizens; it will be founded on freedom, justice and peace as imagined by the prophets of Israel; it will guarantee equality in the social and political rights of all its inhabitants, regardless of religion, race or sex; it will ensure freedom of religion, conscience, language, education and of culture; it will also protect the Holy Places for all religions; and it will remain faithful to the principles of the Charter of the United Nations.

THE STATE OF ISRAEL is willing to work with the agencies and the representatives of the United Nations in putting into work the resolution of the General Assembly of 29 November 1947, and will work towards the economic union of all of Eretz-Israel.

WE APPEAL to the United Nations to help the Jews in the creation and development of its State and to receive the State of Israel into the comity of nations.

WE APPEAL – in the middle of the current attack against us – to the Arab citizens of the State of Israel to maintain peace and work together in the creation of the State of Israel based on full and equal citizenship and due representation in all of its temporary and permanent institutions.

WE EXTEND our hand to all the neighbouring states and their inhabitants in peace and good neighbourliness, and appeal to them to develop bonds of cooperation and mutual assistance with the sovereign Jewish people established in their own land. The State of Israel is ready to do its share in a mutual effort for advancement in the Middle East.

WE APPEAL to the Jewish people throughout the Diaspora to support the Jewish people of Eretz-Israel in the jobs of immigration and development and to stand by them in the fight for the realization of the old dream - the redemption of Israel.

PLACING OUR TRUST IN THE "ROCK OF ISRAEL," WE WRITE OUR SIGNATURES ON THIS PROCLAMATION AT THIS SESSION OF THE PROVISIONAL COUNIL OF STATE, ON THE SOIL OF THE HOMELAND, IN THE CITY OF TEL-AVIV, ON THIS SABBATH EVE, THE 5TH DAY OF IYAR, 5708 (14 May, 1948).

David Ben-Gurion